Ending the *Homework Hassle*

SO?

D0406112

OCT 2 5 2005

Ox ⅟₀₈

OCT 2 5 2005

ENDING THE
Homework Hassle

Understanding, Preventing, and Solving School Performance Problems

John K. Rosemond

3 1336 06997 6844

Andrews and McMeel
A Universal Press Syndicate Company
Kansas City

Ending the Homework Hassle
copyright © 1990 by John K. Rosemond.
All rights reserved. Printed in the United States of America.
No part of this book may be used or reproduced in any
manner without written permission except in the case of
reprints in the context of reviews. For information write
Andrews and McMeel, a Universal Press Syndicate Company,
4520 Main Street, Kansas City, Missouri 64111.

Designed by Edward King.

Library of Congress Cataloging-in-Publication Data
Rosemond, John K., 1947-
    Ending the homework hassle : understanding, preventing, and
solving school performance problems / John K. Rosemond.
        p.   cm.
    ISBN 0-8362-2807-3 : $9.95
    1. Homework. 2. Education—United States—Parent
participation. I. Title.
LB1048.R67   1990
649'.68—dc20   90-37808
                                                        CIP

    04 05 BAM 22 21 20 19 18

Attention: Schools and Businesses
Andrews and McMeel books are available at quantity discounts
with bulk purchase for educational, business, or sales promotional
use. For information, please write to: Special Sales Department,
Andrews and McMeel, 4520 Main Street, Kansas City, Missouri
64111.

*To Willie, for believing enough
to put up with
this book-a-year jazz.*

Contents

Acknowledgments and Appreciations

To Donna Martin, Tom Thornton, Jean Lowe, Patty Dingus, Diane Galante, Lee Salem, and all the other good folks at Andrews and McMeel and Universal Press Syndicate, for your dedicated support of my "mission."

To everyone at the Knight-Ridder Wire, the *Charlotte Observer*, and the other papers that carry my column, for your support and affirmation over the years.

To Paul and David and everyone at *Better Homes and Gardens* magazine, for having the moxie to roll the dice.

To Henry and Mindy Young, Anda Cochran, Barbara McCarthy, Candy Grooms, Tim and Mimi Helms, and Matthew Alexander, for your time and helpful editorial suggestions.

To Ellen Sorrels, for hours of typing and your many helpful comments. To Don Van Schenck, M.D., for more than I can say.

To all of the parents and children in my private practice who, over the years, were instrumental in helping these ideas take shape.

To the Rolling Stones, who gave so generously of their time and talents during the writing of this book in the fall of 1989, for providing just enough diversion to help me maintain my sanity. It's only rock 'n' roll, but I like it!

To the "family" at the Out Island Inn, Georgetown, Exuma, Bahamas, and especially to Willie, Eric, Amy, John, Charmaine, John Jr., Derrick, Charlie, Mara, Gove, Javier, Cindy, John, Lynn, Eric, Peter, and the Groupers: Deerfield Ron (the Deerfield Don), Tony "Slowhand" Milo, Orlando Slim, and Charlie "Boom-Boom" Habeeb, not to mention the lovely Grouperettes, for bringing me safely back to earth after the book was finished. Conchy Joe loves ya!

Ending the *Homework Hassle*

Introduction

These days, I spend much of my professional time traveling around the country making presentations to and putting on workshops for various parent and professional groups.

If I'm talking about school performance issues, I will, at some point, ask for a show of hands from those parents who assist their children with homework on a regular, almost daily, basis. Typically, more than half the people in the audience raise a hand. I then ask for a show of hands from those people whose parents assisted them with *their* homework as frequently. Very few hands ever go up.

In my clinical practice, problems over homework—and schoolwork in general—bring more parents to my office than any other single issue. A sampling of typical complaints:

"Billy won't do his homework unless I'm sitting right there with him, pushing him along every step of the way."

"I know she can do it on her own, she just won't! I end up doing a lot of it for her, which I realize is wrong. But if I didn't do it, it wouldn't get done."

"He hides his homework from us, then tells us he's done it when he hasn't!"

"She does nothing in class, brings her unfinished work home, and we work on it together until all hours of the night."

All this complaint, this brouhaha, this general gnashing of teeth over homework, is relatively new. Veteran teachers—ones who've been teaching thirty years or more—tell me that whereas there was always an occasional child who tried to get away with not doing his homework, the problem has never been so widespread. In any given elementary school classroom today, there are at least five kids who can't be trusted to do their homework on their own. At home, their parents must "stand over them" while they do homework at the kitchen table or the homework won't get done. At school, their teachers usually do the same. Not surprisingly, homework problems are even more common in junior and senior high school. Clearly, adults are hassling with homework more than ever before.

Why? What in the last thirty or forty years has happened to turn homework into such a major hassle for so many people? Why are so many more parents directly involved in the getting-done of homework these days than was the case just a few decades ago? It's not because school itself has gotten harder. In fact, academic standards have actually been downgraded since the early 1950s.

It's not because parents are that much more available to help. In the 1950s and early 1960s, relatively few women were in the work force. Like mine, most mothers were at home to greet and supervise their children after school. And yet, consistent with my experience, my peers tell me that their mothers didn't provide more than occasional guidance where homework was concerned. The kids of my generation came home, went outside to play, came inside when dinner was ready, did their homework, and then played with siblings, worked on hobbies, or watched television until bedtime. If we needed our parents' help, we asked and they helped (if they felt the help was *truly* needed, that is) and then we went back to our rooms and finished our homework—*on our own*.

It's not because teachers are assigning more homework. Whereas teachers assigned more in the 1980s than they did in the 1970s, when homework fell out of favor in many educational circles, my seasoned sources tell me that today's teachers are assigning no more than they did when I was in school. If my kids are any indication, homework shouldn't consume any more of a child's time today than it did thirty years ago.

So, why then? In order to understand why parents are more involved in homework than ever before, and why homework is so much more of a hassle than it's ever been, take note of the fact that today's parents—especially middle- and upper-middle-class parents—are overly involved in nearly *everything* their children do. Parents are more involved in their children's social lives than ever before. Parents are more involved in their children's recreational lives than ever before. And parents are more involved in their children's academic lives than ever before.

The end result of all this well-intentioned involvement is that parents wind up taking responsibility for major aspects of their children's learning—whether it's learning how to get along with others, learning how to choose friends, learning how to occupy time, learning how to read, write, and do arithmetic, or learning from their mistakes, wherever and whenever they occur. That last one's the Big Bugaboo. Today's parents seem convinced that, if left to their own devices, children will make mistakes. To prevent those mistakes from occurring, and to prevent themselves from looking like bad parents when they do occur, today's well-meaning but misguided parents meddle in things they have no business meddling in at all.

Actually, if left to their own devices, children *will* make mistakes. That's good, because most truly valuable learning takes place by trial-and-error, with emphasis on the *error*. If, therefore, the error is prevented, so is the learning. It's as simple as that.

Once upon a time not long ago, parents accepted that reality. As my stepfather used to tell me, "There are certain things you're going to have to learn *the hard way.*" Today's parents, by and large, seem determined to prevent *the hard way* from ever happening. They reason that collisions with *the hard way* make children temporarily frustrated and unhappy (true). Frustration and unhappiness result in damage to a child's self-esteem (false). Good parents don't sit idly by and let damage occur to a child's self-esteem (true). Good parents, therefore, should do everything within their power to prevent collisions between children and *the hard way.* Oh, boy. The truth is that temporary bouts of frustration and unhappiness, the natural consequences of collisions with *the hard way*—otherwise known as *reality*—are forces for learning and change—otherwise known as *growth*, otherwise known as *self-esteem*.

Sometime between 1950 and the present, there occurred a radical, if insidious, shift in our attitudes toward the raising of children. During that same time, the language of childrearing changed to reflect this shift. Raising children became *parenting*, a much more serious, high-tech word. Self-confidence became *self-esteem*, a much more fragile, sensitive word. Along the way, we created a new profession—parenting expert. Prior to this, mind you, there were people among us who were experts at raising children. We called them "Maw-Maw" and "Paw-Paw" and silly things like that. The new parenting experts have fancy degrees and fancy offices. They sit behind big desks and say serious things while stroking their chins. And with their "help," the upbringing of children became not just a *bigger* deal than it had ever been before, but a more *difficult* deal as well.

The parenting experts told parents that the more involved they were with their children, the better parents they were, and the bigger and stronger their children's self-esteem would become. So involved they became. And the more involved they became, the more anxious they became about mistakes that either they or their children might make. So, hoping to prevent mistakes, they appropriated huge chunks of responsibility—socially, recreationally, academically—that rightfully belonged to their children. And the more responsible parents became, the less responsible children became (of course!). And the less responsible children became, the harder raising them became (of course!).

Under the circumstances, it's not at all surprising that homework has become such a big deal for so many of today's parents, and no more surprising that so many children can't be trusted to do their homework on their own. But, take heart, because this is a book designed to remedy all that. This is a book written to take the hassle out of homework, to put the ball in the proper court, to help children learn to paddle their own canoes, and all that proverbial stuff.

Six years ago, I wrote two newspaper columns on homework. Over the next three months, I received close to ten thousand requests for reprints of those columns. That told me that what I was experiencing in my office was not unique to Gastonia, North Carolina. It was nationwide. That's when I began putting this book together.

Before it became a book, however, it was a workshop entitled either "Helping Your Child Succeed in School" (parent version), or "Working with Parents of At-Risk Students" (teacher version), which I've conducted in hundreds of locations around the country. Doing that workshop helped me refine the material, put me in closer touch with the types of problems parents and teachers were experiencing around the issue of homework, and helped me discover creative solutions to those problems. In a sense, major portions of this book were "written" by those workshop audiences.

In the meantime, several other books on homework have been written. One says responsible parents help their children with homework on a nightly basis and gives step-by-step, play-by-play directions for doing just that. Not this book. This book will help you keep a safe distance from your child's homework.

Another book talks at great academic lengths about learning styles and learning theory. It goes on and on about such esoteric blah-blah-blah as the right brain versus the left brain, auditory processing, visual-motor sequencing, and so on. This book isn't like that either. It's not academic. It's not complicated. It's not theoretical. It's not hard to read. It's practical, down-to-earth stuff. The kind grandma used to dispense.

All of the other how-to-help-your-kids-with-homework books currently on the bookshelves encourage lots of parent involvement. The one you're holding isn't a book about getting involved. It's about coaching from the sidelines, as opposed to getting swept up in the action on the field.

Am I calling for something radical? No, just a return to the sanity of a time not so far past, when parents didn't get overly involved in things like homework, and children did their homework.

Am I advocating that parents take no interest whatsoever in school matters? Not at all. In fact, I believe parents should take *great* interest in school matters. I'm simply drawing a line, hopefully clear, between interest and involvement, between consulting and participating, between managing and manipulating.

The last thing you should know about this book, before you begin the easy task of reading it, is that the plans and programs contained within were all developed, tested, and refined on real children, beginning with my own and including hundreds of others whose parents have come to me pulling their hair out, screaming for help because of homework hassles. Except for those who didn't follow my advice, along with those who, because of one of Mother Nature's dirtier tricks (of which I, too, am a partial victim), would have lost their hair anyway, none of those parents are bald today.

For that reason, I can honestly say, "This stuff works!" If you work at it, it'll work for you, too.

Chapter One

The Hassle

This book has its beginnings in a story. It's a story that's been told to me by literally hundreds of parents over the past ten years or so. It comes in several versions, but it generally goes something like this:

"Billy is in the third grade and we're having a problem getting him to do his work. His teacher has to almost stand over him to get him to do anything at all during the day; otherwise, he'll just sit and piddle or talk to the children around him. As a result, he's supposed to bring home not only whatever homework has been assigned, but also the classwork he's failed to finish. In the past, however, he's lied to us about whether or not he has homework and how much, so before he leaves school, he's to write his assignments down in an assignment notebook and take the list to his teacher, who checks it for accuracy and initials it.

"When he gets home, the first thing I do is go over the assignments with him, making sure he knows what he's supposed to do and that he has the necessary books and materials. Sometimes, however, he forgets—at least he *says* he forgets—to write his assignments in the notebook, and I guess the teacher gets caught up in other things and doesn't ask to check it, in which case I either have to rely on his word or call another parent. I've even called the teacher at home, and there have been more than a few times when I've driven back up to the school to get books or other things he's forgotten.

"So (heavy sigh), once we get everything together, I sit

him down at the kitchen table, where I can supervise and provide whatever help he needs, and we get started. Except he does the same thing with me he does in class: He just sits and piddles unless I'm right there. So I end up sitting with him, explaining the work step-by-step, and sometimes—I have to admit—dictating things to him so all he has to do is write down what I'm saying. I know that means I'm sort of doing his work for him, but sometimes I just can't help it, I get so frustrated waiting for him to put pencil to paper.

"I mean, he sometimes acts like he doesn't have a brain. We go over a problem on Monday and I'm sure he knows how to do it, but he draws a blank on Tuesday, so we go over it again, but then it's the same old story on Wednesday. I know he's smart, his teacher knows he's smart, and there isn't anything he *wants* to do that he can't do, but schoolwork just seems to anesthetize his circuits or something. I don't know what it is. All I know is it's driving me slowly nuts. If I manage to survive this with my sanity intact, it'll be a miracle.

"So anyway, from the time Billy gets home until supper—in between trying to cook, answer the phone, and take care of the other kids—I'm helping him with homework. I guess you could say my life isn't my own. Billy's dad gets home around six, at which point we clear the table of books and other homework stuff and set the table for supper. After we finish eating, we clear the table and back come the books.

"You can generally find me helping Billy with his homework until eight o'clock. But wait! Billy has baseball practice after supper on Tuesdays and Thursdays and a piano lesson after school on Wednesday. On those days, we might be up with homework until nine or ten. No joke!

"In the morning, before he leaves for school, I make sure Billy's packed his bookbag properly. I learned my lesson there after having to drive his homework to school a couple of times because he left it at home.

"I just don't understand it. The mothers of other children in his class tell me it takes their kids thirty, maybe forty-five minutes a night to do their homework. It takes us three or four hours. Granted, Billy's got to finish work he should have finished in class, but even that shouldn't keep us at the kitchen table more than an hour and thirty minutes, at most.

"By the time we're done, I'm a wreck. Sometimes I lose my patience and start screaming at Billy, which makes him cry, which makes me feel like a total failure. Then my husband comes in and gets mad at Billy for getting me upset, and I begin defending him, saying it isn't his fault, and it's downhill from there.

"How do I explain all this to myself? Sometimes I think Billy must have some problem, maybe some learning problem or something, but then he does well on the standardized tests they give at the end of the year. Then I think maybe he has low self-esteem and that this is just his way of getting me to pay attention to him. Maybe I haven't paid enough attention to him since the other kids came along. Maybe he feels neglected or something, I don't know. My best friend says Billy's manipulating me, but I don't see how that could be. After all, he's not enjoying our homework sessions any more than I am, so if he's manipulating me, he's sort of cutting off his nose to spite his face, don't you think?"

And the band plays on.

The Names of the Games

There are certain key elements to this scenario which, although the specific details may be different from one child to the next, are present nearly every time the story is told.

First, there's "The Great Homework Hunt," also known as "Homework Hide-and-Seek." This is where Mom (it's almost always Mom) goes through great contortions trying to figure out just exactly what work Billy (or Susie) is supposed to do that evening. Mom rifles through Billy's bookbag in search of clues, she combs his notebooks for evidence, she calls other parents, she calls the teacher, she consults Billy's astrological chart. All the while, Billy just sits there. Waiting.

Next, we have an prime example of what I call "Parenting by Helicopter." Note that Mom has Billy do his homework at the kitchen or dining room table so that she can "supervise," meaning she hovers over him, prodding and bribing and cajoling and directing and doing things for Billy that he's perfectly capable of doing for himself, all the while becoming more and more flustered.

Meanwhile, Billy plays "Duh, I'm Dumb." He acts, in his mother's words, "like he doesn't have a brain." He forgets things that've been drilled into his head for days, he can't think of anything to write to an instruction as simple as "Write a sentence containing the words *I, sat,* and *table.*" His writing hand moves only slightly quicker than a fly in molasses. He adds when he should subtract, circles when he should underline, and generally acts like he's taken an overdose of Valium.

This all culminates in "The Homework Marathon," in which thirty minutes of homework takes three hours. As I write, the formula for finding the actual length of the marathon is being worked on by the same team of astro-physicists that finally answered the question, "Who put the bomp in the bomp shu bomp shu bomp?"

Finally, Billy and his parents play "We're a Bunch of Bananas." After beating her head against the same old brick wall for hours, Mom has a meltdown, which causes Billy to begin wailing, which makes Dad furious, which causes Mom to get between Dad and Billy, which makes Dad even more furious, which ruins everybody's evening, if it wasn't already ruined, and then everyone goes to bed and has horrible nightmares in which they're being chased by huge erasers, bent on rubbing them out.

The PG-13 Version

In the junior high and high school versions, Billy's parents don't know anything is wrong until midterm reports come in. Sometimes, however, Billy intercepts the mail and the reports never show up. Billy's parents, thinking no news is good news, don't ask any questions. If his parents *do* manage to get their hands on the midterm reports, Billy invents all sorts of excuses to explain the poor grades.

He says things like, "I just made an A on a test that wasn't included in the report, so, like, chill out, 'cause my report card grade should be at least a B." Then he gives his parents this "you are really pitiful" look.

Or, "Everybody got bad midterm grades because of this one really hard test that nobody passed, but the teacher said he might not even count that test for the final grade, so this is really no big deal, ya know?"

Or (my favorite), "Oh, that? Well, yeah, like I didn't hand in this one assignment—I mean I did it and all, but I like let Scott see it cause he didn't understand it, and he lost it. Anyway, the teacher gave me a zero, but it's like just a warning 'cause she's lettin' me do some extra credit stuff and so my report card grade's gonna be, like, fine. So, cool your jets, okay?"

Every day, as soon as Billy comes home from school, his mother asks, "Did everything go well in school today?"

"Sure," Billy mumbles.

"Do you have any homework?"

"Not much," Billy mumbles.

"Any tests you need to study for?"

"Nope."

"Well, let me know if you need any help," says Mom.

"Sure," Billy mumbles.

Later, as Billy heads out the door, Mom asks, "Homework done?"

"Uh-huh," Billy grunts.

Several weeks later, the next report card comes out and the grades aren't any better and Billy promises he'll do better, except maybe in Algebra because, "My teacher doesn't like me." If the grades don't improve, and his parents threaten to restrict him, he says, "If you restrict me, you'll take away the only reasons I have for doing good work in school." For some reason, this actually makes sense to some parents. A sure sign of premature senility.

Or, certain grades on the report card have been carefully altered. Most junior high and high schools have "grade doctors" that do this for a living. D's become B's, F's become A's. Parents who fail to notice this need to have their eyes examined.

Billy's parents go talk to the guidance counselor, who promises to meet with Billy on a regular basis to make sure he's keeping up with his work. She also says she'll check in every Friday with Billy's teachers to see how he's doing and make sure he gets whatever extra help he needs. Billy "forgets" his first meeting with the counselor. She chases him down and schedules another, which he can't make because "something important" came up at the last minute and, uh, well, you know the rest.

A Question of Accountability

The basic question, over which there appears to be much confusion, is, "Whose homework is it anyway?"

It's Billy's right? Right! Except no one's acting like it is. Billy's parents, teacher, and (in the junior high/high school version) guidance counselor have, without realizing what they're doing, and certainly with the very purest of intentions, appropriated responsibility for Billy's school performance—responsibility that belongs to Billy. In so doing, they've taken Billy's problem—his failure to do his schoolwork—away from Billy and made it their own, emotionally and otherwise.

PROOF: When Billy fails to do his schoolwork, who gets upset? Billy's parents and, to a lesser extent, Billy's teacher or teachers, that's who! Billy doesn't get upset at all.

PROOF: When Billy fails to do his schoolwork, who *does* something about it? Again, Billy's parents, teachers, and guidance counselor. They monitor, supervise, hover, confer, and ask lots of neurotic questions like, "Is your homework done?" Billy does nothing. He dodges, deceives, dinks around, acts dumb, and dishes up a lot of dookey whenever he's confronted with the facts.

As things stand, Billy has absolutely no reason to change his ways. He's "off the hook." And as long as people continue to do for Billy what he ought to do (and is certainly capable of doing) for himself, as long as people continue feeling for Billy what he ought to be feeling about himself (mad, frustrated, guilty) he has complete permission to continue being irresponsible.

Every night, Monday through Thursday, homework occupies center stage in Billy's family. It becomes the primary focus of family activity. It attracts more energy and attention than any other issue. Everything stops, or is left to just stumble along, until Billy finishes his homework. His parents' marriage stops, domestic responsibilities are done catch-as-catch-can, the other children are left to fend for themselves. And who do we find sitting complacently at the center of the homework hurricane? Billy. He's the central character in this nightly soap opera. Moreover, he's both the victim and the villain, depending on whether his mother is feeling guilty or angry. Most confusing!

Homework doesn't belong at center stage in a family. Homework doesn't *deserve* this much attention. When it's allowed to work its way into the spotlight, there will be nothing but trouble. People will lose track of whose homework it is, and as in the case of Billy's mother, their typical attempts to solve the homework problem will only make it worse.

The Parent Trap

Some people—even some professionals—might say that Billy is using homework to "manipulate" and get attention from his parents. But the fact that a certain behavior results in the child *getting* attention doesn't mean the child is *seeking* attention. Besides, young children aren't generally capable of thinking in sophisticated and insightful terms about themselves and the impact their behavior is having on others. They don't sit around conspiring against their parents, devising clever ways of pulling the proverbial rug out from under them.

Problems of this sort usually have their roots early in the child's development. In most instances, they stem back to precedents set before the child was four years old. The manner in which parents handle certain issues when they first come up in the parent-child relationship not only sets the tone for how these same issues will be handled in the future, but also determines how ongoing they will be. If, in particular, parents set dysfunctional precedents concerning responsibility and autonomy—the two issues most germane to the subject of homework—then these issues will keep coming up in the parent-child relationship. Each time the issue comes up, it's likely to wear a new "disguise."

Let's speculate, for example, that when it was time for Billy to learn to use the toilet, his parents hovered anxiously over him, worrying about "accidents." Their hovering interfered with Billy's ability to take autonomous responsibility for this important learning process. The more they hovered, therefore, the more accidents he had. The more accidents he had, the more anxious his parents became, and the more they hovered.

Unbeknownst to Billy's parents, they were not only their own—and Billy's—worst enemy, they were also building a trap that would ensnare all of them whenever the issues of responsibility and autonomy arose in the parent-child relationship. When these issues first came up—as they did with toilet training—no one learned to handle them in a functional manner. So when they came up again, although in different form, people just fell back into their same old dysfunctional ways.

When it was time for Billy to start picking up after himself around the house and keep his room orderly, he started having "accidents." The more accidents he had, the more his parents hovered and nagged and nothing was accomplished. To this day, he still does not pick up after himself or keep his room straight. Who does? Guess.

When it was time for Billy to begin getting himself up in

the morning and dressing himself on time for school, he started having "accidents." He dinked around in the morning, which aroused his parents' anxiety, which caused them to begin hovering, which resulted in nothing getting accomplished. To this day, he still does not get up by himself and prepare himself properly and on time for school. Who gets him up? Who makes sure he gets to school on time? Guess.

So, when it was time for Billy to accept responsibility for his homework, guess what? Right! He started having "accidents." And 'round and 'round go Billy and his parents in the same old rut. This is not manipulation. This is not attention-seeking behavior. This is a soap opera, and no one knows quite how they got into the roles they're playing. No one knows exactly what they're doing, no one knows why they're doing it, and no one knows how to stop.

In this case, I put Billy's mother in the central role because I wanted to illustrate a truth about our culture, which is that mothers are more likely to feel personally responsible for their children's problems than are fathers. To the average, middle-class American mom, it's taken pretty much for granted that if her child fails to measure up to one standard or another—whether behavioral, social, or academic—it's in some way indicative of a failing or inadequacy on *her* part. You see, our culture sends some very dysfunctional messages to women, and right up there at the top of the list is, "Once you have children, you're only as good as your kids are well behaved, do well in school, achieve social success, and so on."

This message is operational even if a woman with children works outside the home. To see the truth in what I'm saying, ask yourself, "What do we call a woman who has children and works outside the home?" The answer, of course, is "working mother." Let that sink in a minute. Do you begin to get a feel for the implications of that seemingly innocuous phrase? Now, ask yourself, "What do we call a man who has children and works outside the home?" We don't call him a "working father," do we? We call him a "guy with a job"—a plumber, a doctor, a mechanic, or whatever.

The phrase "working mother" says, "If you're a woman with children and you decide to work outside of your home, your primary obligation is still to your kids." It also says, "By choosing to work outside the home, you must understand and accept that you are depriving your children of something that no one else can provide adequately for them—*your* attention."

As a result, in order to expiate the guilt that comes from deciding to do something for herself, something independent of her roles as wife and mother, when the "working mother" gets home from her job, she beats herself into what I call a "quality-time frenzy" in the name of making up to her children what she thinks she has so selfishly deprived them of for the past eight or nine hours.

And so, to Billy's mother, whether she has an outside job or not, Billy's performance in school is a direct reflection of her own competency as his so-called "primary parent."

Because mothers tend to measure their self-worth in terms of their children's behavior and performance, they're also the first to panic when things go wrong, because their children's mistakes and problems give rise to the fear that they might be bad mothers. Their ensuing panic drives counterproductive behavior of the kind Billy's mother is displaying. And while mom panics, dad is all too likely to sit in the den, watching television or reading the newspaper. This is not *his* problem, or so say the messages we send to dads. He's responsible for maintaining his family's standard of living, not seeing to it that the kids get their homework done.

Don't misunderstand me. I'm not suggesting that dad should be an equally active participant in the panic over Billy's homework. Quite the contrary. I'm suggesting that the whole situation is quite convoluted and needs a major overhaul. Everyone's role in this drama needs to change, and until that happens, everyone will stay in the same rut, night after night after night after night after night.

How to Slice a Banana

Bear with me while I tell another story, this time about a thirty-five-year old named Myron: Myron likes to play golf on the weekends. He's just your basic weekend golfer and, like many of his breed, he's afflicted with what's known as the "banana-ball" or slice.

A slice, for the uninitiated, is when the ball, instead of traveling straight toward the target, curves hugely to the right (or left, in the case of a left-handed golfer) and lands in tall grass, woods, water, or beyond the out-of-bounds markers.

Myron's solution to the banana-ball is simple: He aims to the left. This increases the likelihood that the ball, after traveling its wayward course, will come down in the general vicinity of the target. In other words, instead of going to a golf professional for help in discovering the *cause* of the slice and truly *correcting* it, Myron simply *compensates* for it.

The compensation of aiming left doesn't address the problem, but it does conceal, to one degree or another, its consequences. Myron still has a banana-ball, but if he's lucky, it bananas where he wants it to banana, so he's generally satisfied.

The problem is that as long as Myron compensates for his tendency to slice, the worse the slice is going to get. Over time, you see, the problems that are causing the slice become more and more embedded in Myron's grip, swing, or stance. As those problems become habit, Myron must aim further and further left, compensating for a slice that's getting more and more bananas.

Myron finally sees the light and consults a golf professional about his banana ball. The golf professional takes Myron out to the practice tee and has him aim straight toward the target.

"But," protests Myron, pointing to the right, "I'll just hit it over that fence."

"That's all right," answers the pro. "Just bear with me."

Myron swings and hits the ball over the fence.

"See," he says, with noticeable irritation.

"I see," says the pro. "Now, hit another one."

The next ball goes over the fence, too. And the next and the next and the next. Meanwhile, the professional makes a few small adjustments in Myron's grip. Sure enough, the slice becomes slightly less pronounced, but it's still there.

After about thirty minutes, the professional says, "Come back in a week, but if you play a round of golf before the next time I see you, I want you to promise that you'll always aim straight at the target, no matter how badly you're hitting the ball or how badly you're scoring."

"I promise," says Myron.

The next time Myron plays golf, he follows the pro's advice, loses a dozen balls, shoots the worst score of his life, and has no fun at all. The next time he sees the pro, he's fuming.

"See what your advice has done to my game," he yells, waving the score card in the pro's face.

"Myron," says the pro, calmly, "didn't anyone ever tell you that things get worse before they get better?"

The golf pro has brought Myron face-to-face with not just one, but three facts of life:

• First, you cannot *correct* a problem and *compensate* for it at the same time. Compensation and correction are two mutually exclusive, incompatible strategies. In order to correct a problem that you've been previously compensating for, you must first stop any and all compensations.

• Second, the longer you compensate for a problem, the worse it gets. Compensating only hides the consequences of the problem while allowing the problem to worsen.

• Third (and therefore), when you stop compensating for a problem, when you stop hiding the consequences of it and get down to the business of truly *correcting* it, things get worse before they get better.

When you stop compensating for a problem, it forces the problem to shed its disguise and come out of hiding. Now that it's fully visible, it looks really bad, for sure. Worse than ever, in fact, because you're no longer concealing its consequences. Ah, but the good news is that now that the problem's out in the open, you can begin to solve it! You can't solve a problem unless it's completely out in the open, now can you? Of course not! So not only do problems get worse before they get better, they absolutely *must*.

Sometimes, bringing a problem out in the open is all you need to do to solve it. As some wise man once said, "The best cure for a problem, any problem, is sunlight."

Back to Billy

Billy's parents are doing same thing about Billy's failure to do his classwork/homework that Myron was doing about his banana ball. Instead of addressing the root cause of the problem, they—along with his teacher and guidance counselor— are *compensating* for it. His teacher is checking and initialing Billy's assignment notebook; his mother goes on "The Great Homework Hunt" and then makes sure Billy has everything he needs to do his work; she orchestrates "The Homework Marathon" and makes sure the homework's in his bookbag before he leaves for school in the morning. In the junior high version, the guidance counselor runs around like the proverbial headless chicken because Billy won't cooperate with the "help" she's extending to him. All of these are examples of "aiming left."

And the longer everyone compensates, the more bananas everyone—with the notable exception of Billy—gets, and the worse the problem becomes because the root cause isn't being addressed.

What's the root cause? To put it in simple terms, Billy's lazy. Call it irresponsibility, if you prefer a bigger word. And the more everyone else hovers and takes on his responsibilities, the more lazy/irresponsible Billy becomes.

Likewise, in order to cure Billy's problem, everyone's going to have to stop compensating for it—everyone's going to have to let it come out in the open, exposed to the curative powers of the sun. That means everyone must stop being responsible for Billy's homework and let Billy be responsible for it on his lonesome. In other words, everyone is going to have to do absolutely nothing. They're going to have to stop aiming left.

I can hear some of you saying, "Do nothing? You must be kidding!"

That's right, do nothing, at least for a time. Let the problem come out in the open. Stop trying to hide it. Remember the first of our three facts of life? You can't correct a problem and compensate for it at the same time. No one will know just exactly what the problem looks like until it can be seen in its awful entirety. The teacher needs to stop checking Billy's assignment notebook. If he wants to write his assignments down, fine. If not, that's fine too. His mother needs to stop going on "The Great Homework Hunt," stop hovering, stop orchestrating "The Homework Marathon," stop working up to "We're a Bunch of Bananas," and stop making sure his bookbag is correctly packed in the morning. In short, stop being such a responsible parent and let Billy come to grips with some responsibility for a change. It's high time, wouldn't you all agree?

"But won't that just give Billy permission to be as lazy as he wants?"

Now you're getting it! Remember, the problem *has* to get worse before it can get better. That's the way it is in golf and that's the way it is in homework and that's probably the way it is in all of life, wherever and whenever people have been compensating for problems instead of doing what they must to truly solve them.

At this point, there are no doubt many of you out there who think I'm completely off my rocker. You're shaking your heads, making little noises of confusion and disgust, you may even be a moment or two away from throwing this book in the trash. If you're upset with me, it's only because I'm disturbing the compensations that have become embedded in your thought processes. You see, for every compensation that takes place in a person's behavior, there is a parallel compensation in his or her thinking. As I disturb those compensations, things get worse before they get better. In other words, you get upset. If you'll bear with me, however, things *will* get better. Slowly. Remember, Rome wasn't built in a day, and Myron did eventually learn how to hit the ball straight.

Why Is Homework Important?

Good question, and before we go any further, it needs an answer.

Homework is important for reasons that are obvious and reasons that are not so obvious. Unfortunately, most people—teachers and parents alike—see no further than the obvious.

The immediate, obvious aim of assigning a child homework is to provide that child with an opportunity to practice and strengthen academic skills. By devoting adequate time to homework, the child stands a better chance of making good grades. Right? Right!

But homework is important for reasons other than good grades. Homework can and should be a character-building experience, a stepping-stone toward emancipation. Managed properly by teachers and parents who have an appreciation for its "hidden values," homework can help a child become equipped with certain very essential emotional and behavioral skills, skills he will eventually need to successfully negotiate the oftentimes complex demands of adult life. These include the skills of responsibility, autonomy, perseverance, time management, initiative, self-reliance, and resourcefulness.

Let's take a closer look at each of those seven attributes, which I call "The Seven Hidden Values of Homework," beginning with . . .

RESPONSIBILITY: The ability to assume "ownership" of that which rightly belongs to you, to fulfill your obligations, to not hesitate to pick up the ball when it bounces into your court, to hold yourself fully accountable for both your mistakes as well as your successes. Homework is a responsibility that rightfully belongs to the child, not the parents. When parents get too involved, they set the process on its head. The "lessons" get done, but the real lesson doesn't get learned.

AUTONOMY: To be self-governing, to stand on your own two feet. Homework is the first time someone other than a parent has assigned tasks to the child on a consistent basis. In that sense, homework breaks new ground. The child is now accountable *outside* the family. The manner in which this golden opportunity is managed will either enhance or obstruct the child's gradual emancipation.

PERSEVERANCE: To confront challenge with determination, to strive in spite of difficulties, to complete what you set out to accomplish. If the Little Train that Could had had a mother train who, upon seeing her child struggle up the mountain, got behind and pushed, there would have been no point to the story. Likewise, there's no point to a child doing homework if every time the child becomes frustrated, parents absorb that frustration and make it all better. It's a sad fact that many, if not most, of today's parents act as if one of their primary tasks is that of protecting their children from frustration. They seem to believe that standing aside and letting a child grapple with frustration, especially when the grappling could have been prevented, is neglectful, and perhaps even abusive. Little do they realize that more often than not, making a child's life easier in the present will only make it harder in the future.

TIME MANAGEMENT: The ability to organize time in an effective, productive manner, to complete tasks on schedule without compromising quality. In this regard, it's most unfortunate that most parents tell children when to start their homework, but not when it must be finished. This sets the stage for a nightly homework marathon. Instead of learning to manage time, the child learns to waste it.

INITIATIVE: To be self-motivated and assertive, to be decisive in defining and pursuing personal goals. It boils down to this:

Who decides when it's time for the child to begin his homework? Initiative is like a muscle. If it's exercised, it strengthens. If, on the other hand, other people are assuming initiative for the child, he will not ever develop the strength to exercise it on his own.

SELF-RELIANCE: To have trust and self-confidence in your abilities. Managed properly, homework empowers, affirms, enlarges, fulfills, actualizes, and enables the child's capacity for competence. Mismanaged, it diminishes, deflates, and disables. And there is no in-between.

RESOURCEFULNESS: The capacity to find, invent, or adapt creative means of solving problems. This is the business, the very stuff of being human, isn't it? Homework provides the (but not the *only*) form, the child provides the substance. Assuming everyone can see past the report card, that is.

And to what, pray tell, do those "Seven Hidden Values" add? Why, to *self-esteem*, of course! Homework, therefore, provides children the opportunity to develop positive self-worth— homework's eighth, and most important, "hidden value."

The manner in which the issue of homework is negotiated, managed, and otherwise handled within a family will set certain precedents that will impact greatly on how the child in question responds to future challenges, how the parents respond to future problems, and most importantly, whether or not that child ever fully develops the skills he or she will need in order to establish and enjoy a successful adulthood.

So, for the kids' sake, let's get it right!

Chapter Two

Ending the Hassle

Tom Peters and Robert Waterman are two management consultants who wrote a widely-read and widely-praised book entitled *In Search of Excellence* (Harper & Row, 1982). Although it dealt primarily with the issue of managing people in the workplace, *In Search of Excellence* has application to almost any situation in which one person is found directing or teaching another. Interestingly enough, it is especially relevant to the raising of children.

Peters and Waterman make the point that the most effective managers are *consultants* to the people they manage. They are skilled at delegating responsibility and equally skilled at keeping a respectful distance from those to whom they delegate. They are authority figures who make their knowledge and expertise available to the people they supervise, but they do not hover over them, watching their every move.

They trust that the people they manage can do their jobs properly, and they communicate that trust by not becoming overly involved in their work. They motivate people by gently pushing the limits of their capacity for competence and self-direction. In so doing, they offer them the opportunity to discover the intrinsic rewards of independent achievement.

The consultant-manager's general policy is one of noninterference, and he breaks with this rule only if absolutely necessary. Likewise, where homework is concerned, a parent's proper role is that of *consultant* as opposed to *participant*, and a fine line divides the one from the other. Upon crossing that line, a parent steps into emotional quicksand, and in the ensuing struggles, the deeper that parent sinks.

Parents who participate in the getting-done of homework not only dilute whatever academic learning was intended, but also, and more importantly, enable the child to become dangerously dependent upon their continued presence and help where homework is concerned.

The parent-consultant stands on the sidelines, providing encouragement and support. The parent-participant runs on and off the field, scooping up the child's every fumble. He might even take the ball away if the child so much as *looks* like he's about to fumble. Little does the parent-participant realize that he's actually *causing* the child to fumble. He serves as a constant distraction, and his interference prevents the child from ever feeling confident with the ball.

The parent-consultant is concerned, but relatively detached. He doesn't refuse any reasonable request for assistance, but his interventions are brief, rarely lasting more than a few minutes. One such intervention might be to refer the child's question back to the teacher—a subtle way of reinforcing the teacher's role as final authority where schoolwork is concerned.

The parent-participant, on the other hand, is so emotionally involved in the child's academic career that he winds up appropriating large chunks of it. His child's success or failure as a student confirms his success or failure as a parent, or so he thinks. In effect, the parent-participant is in there pitching for himself first and his child second.

It stands to reason: The more responsibility a parent assumes for homework, the less the child will assume. The more help a parent provides, the more the child will acquire a feeling of helplessness. The harder a parent works to protect a child from failure, the more the child will begin to feel and act like a failure. After all, you don't need to be protected from failure unless you are in danger of becoming one, now do you?

Instead of taking the credit when their children do well in school and feeling guilt when they don't, parent-consultants *assign* their children responsibility, both positive and negative, for their own academic achievements and failures. Above all else, they allow their children to make mistakes, realizing that the most valuable lessons in life are often learned by trial and *error*.

In all these ways, parent-consultants send messages of trust, affirmation, and personal worth to their children, who are, as a consequence, free to explore and expand their capacity for competence and creativity.

Parent-participants, although well-intentioned, are addicted to being overly involved in their children's lives. They live *through* their children and thus take their children's successes and failures very seriously and very personally. They over-direct, over-protect, and over-indulge. They take on responsibility that rightfully belongs to their children, thus robbing them—although unintentionally—of opportunities for growth.

The following chart contrasts these two roles—that of the overly-involved, parent-participant with the appropriately-involved, parent-consultant. Although we're talking specifically about homework, this chart applies to virtually any area of a child's life—social, recreational, and extracurricular—as well as academic. Ask yourself, "How does it apply to me?"

First, the overly-involved parent-participant *hovers* over the child, obsessively preoccupied with the possibility that the child may make a mistake and determined to anticipate and prevent that unthinkable possibility. I call this "parenting by helicopter."

In the act of hovering, the parent-participant *assumes responsibility*, however unwittingly, for the child's academic (or social or recreational or extracurricular) decisions and/or performance. He over-directs, over-manages, and over-controls. This is over-protection in its purest form—trying to protect the child from failure, and one's self from the implication that the child's failure is a reflection of one's own.

The parent-consultant is simply *available*—there to provide help when help is truly needed—but does not impose his

WHICH ONE ARE YOU?

THE OVER-INVOLVED PARENT	THE CONSULTING PARENT
HOVERS	AVAILABLE
ASSUMES RESPONSIBILITY	ASSIGNS RESPONSIBILITY
ENCOURAGES DEPENDENCE	ENCOURAGES INDEPENDENCE
SENDS NEGATIVE MESSAGES	SENDS POSITIVE MESSAGES

presence upon the child. In the non-act of being available, the parent-consultant *assigns* responsibility to the child for his own academic (or social or recreational or extracurricular) decisions and/or performance. And keep in mind that the more responsibility one is made to accept, the more responsible that person will eventually become. Unfortunately, the reverse is equally true.

In the act of hovering, the parent-participant encourages continuing *dependence*, weakens the child's tolerance for frustration, and thwarts the growth of initiative and resourcefulness. What a terrible price for a child to pay because a parent "only wants to help."

In the non-act of being simply and cleanly available, the parent-consultant encourages *independence* and all of the things that go with it, including self-reliance, initiative, self-motivation, resourcefulness, and the like.

In the act of hovering, the overly-involved parent sends a powerful set of *negative messages*. These include, "I don't trust you to do an adequate job of this on your own," and "I doubt that you're even capable of doing this on your own," and "You make me look bad and feel bad when you make mistakes." These are not the intended messages, but they are the *felt* messages, nonetheless; felt deep in the child's psyche, where they grow into feelings of incompetence, helplessness, and guilt. Eventually, they begin to impact upon nearly everything the child attempts. The child may even stop attempting anything at all in a desperate effort to stop the messages from doing their dirty work.

In the non-act of being simply available, the parent-consultant sends an equally powerful set of *positive messages*, including, "You are competent to do this on your own; I trust that you can, I trust that you want to, and I trust that you will." That also lodges itself deep within the child's psyche, where it shines and shines and shines and shines, lighting the way for one accomplishment after another.

The ABC's of Effective Homework Management

Are you convinced yet? Are you ready to extricate yourself from the never-ending, self-defeating, viciously circular trap of participating in your child's homework and get on with the joys—oh, the joys!—of consulting? Are you ready to get out of the homework business? Then read on, because it's as easy as A-B-C!

"A" STANDS FOR "ALL BY MYSELF": The child does his homework in a private, personal place, preferably at a desk in his room, rather than in a public, family place such as the kitchen table. This physical arrangement not only helps define homework as the child's responsibility (one of the "Seven Hidden Values" of homework, remember?), but also helps parents resist the urge to hover. As they say, "Out of sight, out of mind."

Homework done in the kitchen or any other family area quickly becomes a family affair. This virtually guarantees that homework will become a central, if not *the* central, issue in the family for most of the evening. Homework will command family attention, distract family members from other, more important responsibilities (such as being married), and drain energy from the family that might otherwise be available for more creative, productive pursuits (such as communication).

The child who is allowed to do homework at the kitchen table is being handed an opportunity to exercise a unique sort of control over the family. He sits in a position of power, at the center of a potential hurricane which he can set to swirling simply by acting incompetent. And once a child accidentally discovers what havoc he can cause and how much attention he can garner simply by acting incompetent, he will act incompetent more and more often. It is not, mind you, a manipulation. The child doesn't *want* to be incompetent, he doesn't want to pay this price. It's that he hasn't learned how to resist the temptation. In the process, the child becomes increasingly convinced that he is, in fact, incompetent, and that he does, in fact, need his parents' constant assistance to do homework. Furthermore, the attention the child receives is quite literally addicting. The more he gets, the more he thinks he needs, the more he wants. And since the only way to get it (or so he thinks) is to act helpless, he acts increasingly helpless.

So, off to his room he goes!

The parents' first responsibility, relative to this personal, private homework place is to simply see to it that it's stocked with everything the child needs to do his homework on his own. It should, in other words, be self-contained. There should be an ample supply of paper, pencils and/or pens in sufficient quantity, a ruler, glue, tape, and—as they become necessary— a compass, protractor, dictionary, and set of encyclopedias. An older child's desk might even incorporate an L-shaped extension for a computer and printer. The child should be able, in other words, to do his homework without ever leaving the security of his cozy little homework place. This exercises autonomy, which is another of homework's "Seven Hidden Values."

The parents' second responsibility is to see to it that the child's homework place is comfortable. There should be a comfortable chair, one that provides good support to the lower back, and a desk compatible with the child's height. The desk should be no less than eighteen-inches deep by three-feet wide. This provides enough surface area for the child to "spread out" and work on fairly big projects. Needless to say, the child's desk should have its own lamp, preferably one on a "goose-neck" or "swinging arm" so it can be positioned directly over the work being done.

"B" STANDS FOR "BACK OFF": You, the parent, stay out of the child's homework unless the child asks you to get involved. This means that you do not ask unnecessary questions like, "Do you need any help with your homework?" or "How can you do homework with that music playing?" or even "Do you have any homework today?" Furthermore, you don't do unnecessary things like checking to make sure the child is really doing his homework. Not only don't you offer help, you don't rush to the child's rescue if you hear him pounding his desk in frustration. Remember the value of things learned "the hard way."

Now this is not to say that you shouldn't *ever* help, because you can, but only if the child asks. This exercises initiative, yet another of homework's "Seven Hidden Values." Likely as not, however, the child will not ask for help from his room nearly as often as he would ask if he was seated at the kitchen table.

When Willie and I implemented these homework management strategies with our two children, Eric and Amy, we also made a rule that if one of them had a question, he or she had to pick up books, paper, or whatever, and travel downstairs to where we were. "We will not," we told them, "come running upstairs to your beck and call." In other words, the effort involved in getting help belonged completely to the children. Amazing! The average number of requests for help per evening immediately dropped by more than half. This meant the children were putting more effort into any given problem before asking for help. This meant that perseverance—yet another of the "Seven Hidden Values"—was being exercised, and therefore strengthened.

If the child asks for help, and the request is legitimate, then parents can, and should, give help. When they do, it should be for only one of two reasons: First, because the child is "stuck" at some point, has given it his all, and truly needs adult guidance to get un-stuck. Second, because he has finished his homework, but wants someone to critique (check) it. In either instance, parents should limit their involvement to . . .

- *clarifying* or reinterpreting directions;
- *demonstrating* or giving example of a particular procedure;
- *reviewing* or checking work for accuracy, clarity, and adequacy.

Whatever help is rendered should be *brief* and *encouraging*. Parental involvement should rarely last longer than fifteen minutes, with the norm being closer to five. If it looks like fifteen minutes isn't going to do it, then the parents should consider referring the problem back to the child's teacher, yes, *even if that means the child might not complete the work on time.*

If you decide to get involved, observe the following rules of thumb:

Don't provide the child with a shortcut, which simply means you don't do the child's work for him. If he complains he "can't" do the work on his own, that's an appropriate time to say, "Well, then, that simply means you need to ask your teacher to explain this to you a second time and perhaps even give you some individual help during or after school." In so many words, you're saying, "Perhaps you need to pay better attention in class. At the very least, you need to ask necessary questions of your teacher *before* you leave school. I'm not here to do *your* work for you or *her* work for her. If you truly can't, then put the work away. It will wait until tomorrow."

When our two children first began hearing this message from us, it had a curious effect. They complained, they cried, they even accused us of not caring whether they passed or failed, but more often—much more often—than not, the work got done before school the next day. They said, "We can't," to which we said, "Well, we won't," and suddenly they *could*. I've heard the same thing from more parents than I could shake a stick at, whatever that means.

Don't get in over your head, which means you don't go "back to school" for the child's sake. If the child brings work to you which looks, at first glance, like "Greek," don't bang your head against the book trying to learn the subject matter. Don't, in other words, try to be a hero. Nine out of ten times, your best attempts to do so will only succeed at frustrating you along with your child. This is also an appropriate time to refer the child back to his teacher.

Don't get involved in an emotional exchange with your child over homework. If you decide to give help, and your child begins to complain that your explanation isn't clear, or you aren't doing such-and-such the way the teacher said to do it, then just say, "Well, then, I guess this means I'm not the person to be helping you with this. Maybe you should call one of the other kids in the class and ask if they'll explain it to you. If that doesn't work, then I suppose you can always wait until tomorrow and ask your teacher to help you understand it." In other words, you always have the option of refusing to help your child with homework. It's amazing how motivating such a refusal can be, as the following story about my daughter, Amy, illustrates:

●   ●   ●

Upon entering the tenth grade, Amy was invited into advanced geometry. It was her first accelerated placement in math, and it turned out to be somewhat intimidating, at least initially.

The very first night of the new school year, Amy brought her geometry homework to me and, looking quite exasperated, asked for my help. Having been a rather good geometry student in my day and, like most doting dads, unable to pass up an opportunity to impress my daughter, I spent about thirty minutes familiarizing myself with the material and showing her how to work the problems. As understanding dawned, the lines of tension disappeared from her face, and when I finished she gave me a hug and a warm, "Thank you, Daddy."

"Bill Cosby, you ain't got nothin' on me," I thought.

The next night, Amy again brought her geometry homework to me and again I earned a smile and a hug. This scene repeated itself almost every night for the first two weeks of school. I finally woke up to the fact that Amy was leaning increasingly on me to relieve her frustrations over geometry, and that my helpfulness wasn't, in the long run, doing her any favors.

So the next night, as she once again approached me, geometry book in hand, I said, "Amy, I've decided not to give you any more help with geometry, at least not for a while. I think I've helped you get off to a good start and I'm certain you can handle it pretty much on your own from here."

Her face fell, and she stared at me in disbelief. "Daddy," she pleaded, "I've tried to figure it out, and I can't!"

"Well," I replied, "I think you can. They wouldn't have offered the class to you if they didn't think you could handle it."

"But Daddy, everyone's having problems in there. Nobody understands it!"

"That's something all of you need to call to your teacher's attention, then. If you don't understand the material, you can ask your teacher for extra help, or you can ask a student who *does* understand it to explain things to you. But the bottom line, Amy, is that your daddy's not going to take geometry this year."

She gave me a look that would kill and then, with tears welling up in her eyes, ran from the room, a la Sarah Bernhardt. Pausing at the bottom of the stairs, she dramatically announced, "Then I'll just *fail* geometry!"

When that got no reaction, she ran upstairs and, pausing once again on the landing, cried out, "You'd have helped Eric!"

Ah, yes, I should have known. If all else fails, try the old you've-always-liked-him-better routine.

•   •   •

One of the things parenthood has taught me is that you don't necessarily do children any favors by trying to make them happy. I could have continued to cooperate with, and relieve, Amy's anguish over geometry. That would have been, in fact, the *easiest* thing to have done. Instead, I withdrew my support before she became overly dependent upon it. This forced her to exercise, and therefore strengthen, her powers of perseverance.

In so doing, I made her very unhappy. I'm sure that for a time at least, she hated me for it, but then parenthood isn't a popularity contest. Sometimes, in order to promote a child's progress toward self-sufficiency, parents must do highly unpopular things.

I've also learned that it's possible for a parent to say something positive and affirming to a child, and for the child to not like it at all. In this case, I sent Amy a set of very complimentary messages, including "you're competent," "you're smart," and "you can do it on your own." Nonetheless, I made her furious.

She wanted me to say, in effect, "You're absolutely right. You do need my help. You can't do this on your own." The problem is, if you paddle someone else's canoe long enough, they not only never learn to paddle it themselves, they also become convinced that only *you* are capable of paddling it.

Many of today's parents are reluctant to do anything that

results in their children becoming even temporarily unhappy. There are three factors at work here: First, the mistaken belief that unhappiness threatens a child's self-esteem. Second, the fear that their children will feel unloved or—horror of horrors—won't like them. Third, the fear their peers will disapprove of their child-rearing methods.

So they get in lockstep with the crowd and dedicate themselves to the popular cause of keeping their children happy, no matter what the cost. In the process, they unwittingly deprive their children of essential opportunities to develop self-sufficiency, and therefore self-esteem. What these parents fail to realize is that it's often necessary to temporarily threaten a child's happiness in order to promote the lasting reward of good self-esteem.

Oh, yes, I almost forgot about Amy. She must have discovered the joys of paddling her own canoe, because despite the fact that she never again asked for my help, she made straight A's in geometry that year.

"C" STANDS FOR "CALL IT QUITS AT A REASONABLE HOUR": Set an *upper* time limit on homework. In most instances, the child should be responsible for deciding when to begin, but parents should decide when to call "time." The deadline should be consistent, say eight o'clock every evening, but can be temporarily suspended for special projects and when the child needs more time to study for major tests. The shortest route to a nightly homework marathon is to tell a child when to begin but not when he must be done. Setting an upper limit teaches time-management, which is, you will recall, another of homework's "Seven Hidden Values." Since I told a story about Amy a moment ago, it's only fair that I now tell one about her brother:

•   •   •

When Eric, the older of our two children, was in the third grade, his bedtime was at nine o'clock. Supposedly, that is, because about a month into the school year, he devised a clever way of managing to stay up later. When we would tell him it was time for him to start getting ready for bed, he would suddenly "remember" homework that was due the next day.

"How could you forget?" we would ask.

"I don't know," he'd say, "I just did."

"Okay, Eric, but make it snappy."

And the lights in Eric's room would stay on until ten or maybe even eleven o'clock, with us going to his room every fifteen minutes or so asking, "How much longer is this going to take?" and him answering, "I'm almost done."

Finally, after this had gone on for a couple of weeks, Willie and I finally figured out the game and made a rule that he had to finish his homework—regardless how much of it there was—by eight o'clock.

"Eight o'clock is when we all put our responsibilities down, whatever they are, and become a family again," we said. "We're not going to do office work or housework after eight o'clock, and you're not going to do homework.

"If for some reason—like you have a big test or a major project due the next day—you need more time than the deadline allows, you must let one of us know and ask for an extension as soon as you get home from school. If you forget to ask or don't realize you need to ask until later, the answer will be 'No.'"

"Okay! Okay!" he said, which is what they always say.

The next day, Eric brought some books home, but played outside with friends until supper. After supper, he went upstairs to do homework, or so we thought. At eight o'clock, I went up to his room to find him working on a model.

"Hey, big guy," I said, "Mom and I would like you to come downstairs for a while before you start getting ready for bed."

"Oh, wow!" he exclaimed, "What time is it?"

"Eight o'clock," I answered.

"Oh, wow! I've got some homework to do!"

"Oh, wow!" I exclaimed, "I guess you're out of luck."

"Why?" he asked, as if he didn't know.

"Because we made a rule, Eric, and that's the way it's going to be."

"But I forgot!" he cried.

"That's exactly why we made the rule, Eric."

"But Dad, I'll get a zero if I don't have my homework!"

"So be it, Eric. Now come downstairs and spend some time with us."

"Dad!"

"Dad me no dads, Eric. Come downstairs."

"Okay! I'll be down in a minute."

Knowing full-well what Eric's next move in this cat-and-mouse game was going to be, I went downstairs, waited a few minutes, took off my shoes, tiptoed back up to his room and opened the door. He looked up from his desk, where he was working on arithmetic problems.

"Give me your books, Eric," I said.

"Aw, Dad, you gotta be kidding," he whined, "I gotta finish this before tomorrow!"

"Right, and you can get yourself up early in the morning and do it. Or when you get to school, instead of socializing with your friends, you can find a quiet place in the cafeteria and do these problems. Or you can tell your teacher that the reason you don't have your homework is because your parents are nuts and wouldn't let you do it, but you're giving me your books right now and coming downstairs."

"Dad, please," he pleaded, "I just forgot. I'll remember tomorrow, I promise."

"No. Give me the books."

"DAD!"

"Give me the books. They'll be on the kitchen counter in the morning."

Reluctantly, he handed over the books. The next morning, I heard his alarm clock go off at six o'clock. Then I heard him go downstairs and into the kitchen. Then he came back upstairs and closed his door. That night, I went to his room at eight o'clock. He was hunched over a writing assignment.

"Time to put the homework away, Eric."

"Dad, I've got to finish this report. It's taking longer than I thought it would. Then I've got a spelling test to study for, but I'll be in bed by nine, I promise."

"Eric?"

"What Dad?"

"Give me the books."

"Dad, no, I'm not going to, I mean, I can't, I mean, it's not fair, Dad, really, c'mon Dad, please. PLEASE?"

"No."

He ranted. He raved. He gave me the books, but refused to come downstairs. He went to bed at nine o'clock. The next morning, I heard his alarm go off at six. Then I heard him go down to the kitchen. Then he came back upstairs and closed his door.

The next night, he had his homework done at eight o'clock. But that wasn't the end of it. Over the next few weeks, Eric tested the new rule, as any child would, in a number of brilliantly creative ways. And every time, we simply said, "Give us the books."

At last, convinced that we meant what we said, Eric fell into a consistent routine of getting his homework done at, believe it or not, *well before* eight o'clock. He'd come home, change clothes, and go outside until supper, after which he'd retire to his room. He'd usually emerge around seven or seven-thirty. If he had more homework than usual, he'd start on it immediately after school and sometimes be done before supper. In any case, we never again had to confiscate books at eight o'clock. Meanwhile, he passed Introduction to Time Management 101 with flying colors!

•   •   •

I recently passed my homework management plan on to the parents of a fourth-grade boy who had previously been successful at getting his mother to sit through homework with him nearly every night. Predictably, a homework marathon had developed and was consuming the family's evenings.

Complicating matters was the fact that Darrell had been diagnosed as having a learning disability and spent an hour a day in a special education program. This only served to reinforce his parents' belief that he needed lots of help with his studies. Mom viewed her nightly sacrifice, therefore, as absolutely essential. She was convinced that without her support, Darrell would suffer total academic collapse. Needless to say, persuading these folks to implement the ABC's of my homework management program was no small act of salesmanship.

But they did. They set an upper limit of eight o'clock and slowly, but surely, became occasional consultants rather than full-time participants. After some initial displays of helplessness, Darrell began doing his homework pretty much on his own, in his room rather than at the kitchen table as before. At eight, whether he was finished or not, his parents made him put his books aside and prepare for his nine o'clock bedtime. Within several weeks, his teachers reported that Darrell was not only turning in all of his homework and completing more work in school, but that the quality of his work was improving considerably.

Although Mom was much less involved, she continued the practice of calling out Darrell's spelling words on Thursday night, in preparation for Friday's test.

"Is this okay?" she asked during one of our conversations.

I pointed out that she could, as an alternative, purchase an inexpensive cassette recorder and teach Darrell how to make a review tape of each week's spelling words. This would make him more responsible, I said, and more independent, and he might, in the long run, actually do better in spelling.

"I know," his mother said, "but I *like* reading him the spelling words. It makes me feel like I'm doing *something*."

"Then it's okay by me, as long as you enforce the rules otherwise," I said, and that was that, until a month or so later when she told this tale:

One Thursday night, Darrell started watching television after supper and was still watching at eight o'clock. Suddenly, realizing what time it was, he panicked. He jumped up, ran to his room, got his spelling book, and asked his mother to give him his practice test. Mom refused, pointing out that homework time was over. Darrell was beside himself and began insisting that he would surely fail the next day's test and that it would be her fault.

"It was hard," she said, recounting the incident. "There

was a whole hour before his bedtime that I could have helped him, but I didn't."

"So what did he do?" I asked.

"Well," she answered, "the next morning he got up early and studied his words by himself in his room. Then he went to school and used the half-hour between when the bus gets him to school and the first bell to study some more. It was the first time he'd studied them all on his own."

"So how'd he do on the test?" I asked.

"You won't believe this," his mother said, laughing. "He got the first perfect score he'd ever gotten on a spelling test."

In truth, I had no trouble believing it at all. It never fails: The more responsible a child is for his or her school performance, the better the child does in school.

How Much Homework Is Enough?

One of the more unfortunate things the "Back to Basics" movement in education has spawned is an overemphasis on *quantity* where homework is concerned. The following letter, sent to me by the parents of two elementary-age children, illustrates the problem:

> The school our children attend places a great deal of emphasis on homework. Teachers begin assigning homework in the last half of kindergarten and it builds from there. It isn't unusual for a third-grade child to average two hours of homework a night, four nights a week. And that's two hours, mind you, only if the child doesn't dawdle.

An unfortunate situation, but not at all uncommon. In 1983, a presidential commission report on education called ours a "nation at risk." In response, many school systems across the nation embraced the work ethic. In their obsessive zeal to improve their rankings in the standardized-test scores game, they made the mistake of thinking that more is better.

Presumably, the thinking is that learning and retention

take place in direct proportion to the amount of time a child spends practicing a given lesson. There is, in fact, a grain of truth in this, but the point of diminishing returns is reached relatively quickly. Studies show that when someone is learning a large amount of new information or a new skill, it's best to separate the total learning time into several relatively brief practice periods. This is known as "distributive practice" or "distributive learning." In contrast, "massed practice" occurs when learning is expected to take place in one large chunk of time. Assigning fifty division problems when ten would suffice is an example of massed practice.

A major problem with massed practice is that too many learning trials tend to produce an aversive response toward the learning itself. Aversive conditioning results in attempts on the part of the learner to avoid the cause of his or her discomfort.

If the learner is a child and the discomfort is due to excessive homework, avoidance behaviors will include putting it off 'til the last minute, lying about it, acting incompetent, finding numerous excuses to wander off task, staring out the window, and trying to get someone else to shoulder part, if not all, of the load. In short, the very set of problems that comprise the "Homework Hassle."

And not only that, but too much homework can result in a child eventually losing interest in school and motivation for learning altogether. And this, I needn't tell you, is the deepest cut of all.

The latest research on human learning suggests that while homework is basically a worthwhile exercise, it should not demand, during the early elementary grades, much more than thirty minutes per day, on the average (I recommend that homework be introduced in the second half of first grade). Any more than this and returns are likely to diminish. For a fourth-, fifth-, and sixth-grade child, homework should not consume more than forty-five to sixty minutes a day.

This makes good common sense when looked at from a practical standpoint as well. Six hours spent in school and one hour spent on homework amounts to a seven-hour academic day. Considering that an eight-hour work day is standard for adults, seven hours is plenty to expect of a twelve-year-old child.

From seventh grade on, the "heat" can be gradually increased. Most high school students, and especially those on a college-prep track, should be able to tolerate an average of two hours of homework per night, occasionally more. At this point, the increased load begins to prepare youngsters for the more rigorous demands of college.

Questions?

Q: Doesn't a young child—a first-grader, for example— who's never had experience with homework need more initial guidance and parental involvement than you're recommending?

A: Absolutely! Just as an employee needs more supervision and direction while phasing into a new job than he will eventually need, so the young child needs more guidance from parents while making the adjustment to having homework.

Parents need to understand, however, that the initial nature and extent of their involvement in homework will be precedent-setting. Parents who become overly involved from the first will find it difficult to eventually reduce that involvement, while parents who are initially conservative in their involvement will have little problem gradually pulling back.

The first of my homework ABC's doesn't change. Regardless of the child's age or level of experience with homework, homework should be confined to the child's room or some other private place. This makes it clear, from the first, that homework is the child's responsibility, not a family affair.

The second and third of those ABC's change slightly. A homework deadline should be established and enforced from the start. The young child, however, is going to need more structure than a deadline alone will provide. This can be done in one of two ways:

> • Shortly after the child arrives home, parent and child take a few moments to make an inventory of the child's homework assignments. Taking after-school activities and other factors into consideration, the parent should help the child decide when he needs to begin in order to finish before the established deadline. This simple exercise helps the child begin learning how to manage time, which is, again, one of homework's "Seven Hidden Values."
> • The parent sets a consistent time for starting homework as well as a deadline. The actual amount of time should be no more than enough to allow the child to finish before the deadline on the heaviest of homework days. While this approach isn't quite as effective as the one described above at helping the child to learn time management skills, the routine may be more convenient for some families.

Regardless of how it's determined, when the decided-upon "homework time" rolls around, the young child is probably going to need a gentle reminder: "It's seven o'clock, Heathcliff. Does that mean something to you?"

After the youngster retires to his or her homework place, parents should check in ever so often to see how things are coming along. Their involvement, if any, should be brief and encouraging. As it approaches, they should also remind the child of the deadline. When it arrives, they should enforce it.

Q: If parents have been having problems with homework management, and they implement your Homework ABC's, how long should they expect to wait until things begin working?

A: My experience has been that, generally speaking, five out of ten "homework resistant" children will begin the process of rehabilitating themselves some three or four weeks after their parents implement the plan. The actual length of time is a function of how dependent the child has become upon parental participation in his or her homework. If it's still early in the game, and not much dependency has been established, then the child may pick up the ball and run with it almost immediately. If the child has had time to become very dependent upon parental participation, then it's probably going to take several weeks before things begin turning around. During that time, parents should expect things to get considerably worse before they begin getting better.

After parents stop compensating for the child's homework problems and assign responsibility for them to the child, he must first test to see if they really mean what they say. He asks himself, "Are they really going to go through with it? Are they really going to put it all in my lap, or are they just blowing so much hot air, like they've done so often in the past?"

Once having tested his parents resolve for a couple of weeks and having discovered that they do, indeed, intend to give him complete responsibility for the getting-done of homework, then the child must make a critical decision. He must choose between success and failure, between whether he wants to do well in school or not. The choice is now his, and his alone, which it's never been before. Because it's new, and therefore intimidating, he may have to wrestle with it for a while before making a decision. During this decisive struggle, expect the child to act like he's desperately in need of rescue. In other words, expect things to get worse.

Most human beings, given a choice between success or failure, will choose success. Likewise, most children with major homework problems, after three or fours weeks of wrestling and acting like they're going to sink rather than swim, will make the correct choice. They'll begin swimming.

Q: What if the child doesn't make the correct choice? What if, after three or four weeks, it looks like he's choosing failure. What should parents do then?

A: If, after inviting the problem out into the open, it gets worse but shows no sign of taking a turn for the better, then one of two things is going on:

First possibility: So much dependency has accumulated that the child is unable to discharge it on his own. In that case, the parents are going to have to "jump-start the child's motivational motor." In other words, they're going to have to take the bull by the horns and manage the child toward making the correct decision. There are ways of managing children toward making correct, success-oriented decisions without assuming responsibility for their inappropriate behavior. In Chapter Three, "When to Motivate," I'll discuss some of those techniques and give examples of how they can be used to help the problem student. But be patient. Don't jump ahead of me.

Second possibility: There's more to the problem than meets the eye, meaning the child has a problem or problems which need professional attention. These problems include the need for remediation, the need for retention, a learning disability, and/or attention deficit disorder—all discussed in upcoming chapters.

Q: My eight-year-old, who's now in third grade, has required my help with homework since she started school. At first, it was just occasional, but as the work became more difficult, her needs increased to the point that my help is now almost constant. I agree that, under ideal circumstances, parents should be a few steps removed from a child's homework, but certainly there are exceptions. For example, if I were not so involved, my daughter would certainly fail the third grade. Don't you agree it would be irresponsible of me to simply let this happen?

A: Not necessarily. There's a lot to be said for letting the chips fall where they may in situations of this sort. I think I understand your dilemma. You don't want your daughter to "fail" in the sense of having to repeat the third grade. You probably think that "failure" would damage her self-esteem. Your sense of responsibility demands that you do everything within your power to prevent that from happening.

Without realizing it, however, you're digging an ever deepening hole for both yourself and your daughter. The longer you dig, the harder it's going to be to climb out, and the greater the cost of trying to do so.

You think she would fail if you stopped helping her with homework. For the moment, I'm going to accept your terminology and acknowledge that you may, indeed, be right. The question is, "Are you really preventing your daughter from failure, or are you just forestalling the inevitable?" If your daughter isn't presently able to do third-grade work, then perhaps another year in the third grade would be in her best interest. In any case, your taking the third grade for her won't solve the problem. What you're doing is accelerating rapidly toward an inevitable collision with what I call the "Sooner or Later" Principle. A debt is accumulating, and sooner or later, it will have to be repaid.

It's conceivable that you can, with enough effort, get your daughter all the way through high school and into college. Who's going to help her with homework then? Will you hire a full-time tutor to accompany her to her classes and see to it that she gets a degree? Then who will make sure she succeeds in her chosen career? If you want your daughter to learn to stand on her own two feet instead of always looking around for another pair to stand on, then perhaps you need to let her "fail."

Although they are often confused, even by many educators, "failing" a grade and feeling like a failure are two entirely different things. One does not necessarily follow from the other. It's possible for a child to *never* repeat a grade and end up feeling like a failure. It's equally possible for a child to repeat a grade and end up feeling like a winner.

Indeed, your daughter's self-esteem is at stake. Unfortunately, with the way things presently stand, it's at *risk*. The more help you give, the more dependent upon your help your daughter becomes. The more dependent she becomes, the more incapable and inadequate she feels. The more inadequate she feels, the worse she feels about herself, the further her self-esteem falls. The further it falls, the more helpless she will act, and the more she will look toward you to prop her up.

If you really want to help your daughter, then have a psychologist test her to determine the reasons behind her school performance problems and develop a prescriptive remedial plan. It's entirely possible that the problem can be corrected without retaining your daughter in the third grade. Then again, it may be that retention will, at this point, be in her very best interests. In either case, you need to get out of the homework business and let the chips fall where they may. If you don't, there's going to be a rude awakening, sooner or later.

Q: Our children's teachers not only assign lots of homework, but also frequently assign projects that the children can't possibly do without parental help. We don't mind providing occasional assistance, but feel that the extent of our involvement defeats the purpose of these projects. On the other hand, if we don't help, the child will not receive a good grade and will, as a result, almost certainly suffer humiliation and perhaps even ridicule from other students. What do you suggest?

A: I wholeheartedly agree that too much parental participation in projects defeats the purpose of the projects themselves, which should be to give children opportunity to learn how to synthesize a number of smaller learning experiences into a larger whole, establish and pursue long-range goals, and experience the rewards of independent accomplishment. All of this becomes diluted, if not eradicated, when parents become overly involved.

Teachers have no business assigning work that children can't do, for the most part, on their own. Those who do need to be gently reminded that the primary purpose of education is to help outfit children for self-sufficiency. When I was in school, it was clear that parents were *not* to help with projects. If it was obvious that a child had received parental help, his grade was docked. Today, it's taken for granted that parents are supposed to help, and teachers will reward with better grades those children whose parents got involved. This upside-down practice means, in effect, that children who do their projects on their own are punished for exercising initiative and independence and resourcefulness. Not fair!

So, what can you, as a parent do? For starters, you can discuss the issue with other parents, and perhaps even bring it up at a PTA meeting. You and several other parents could form an ad hoc committee to do research on the issue of homework and make recommendations to the school concerning quantity and the advisability of assigning projects that require parental participation.

If you have the courage, you could stop giving your children much help with their projects. You could limit your involvement to consulting and advising, but keep your hands "clean" of the actual doings. That may mean, however, that your children don't get excellent ratings on their projects, in which case, you should tell your children in advance that the grade isn't that important. Tell them that what's important is for them to do their projects pretty much on their own, that they do their best, and that they take pride in what they've done, even if it doesn't win an award.

When we pulled out of our children's projects, we told them, "This may mean that you don't get an excellent grade. It may mean that your project isn't chosen for the science fair. That's certainly not fair, but that's the way things may turn out, nonetheless. We want you to know, however, that if you do a project on your own, and you do your best, then regardless of the grade your teacher gives you, you get an "Excellent" from us. From that point on, whenever they finished a major project, we took them out to the eatery of their choice to celebrate their independent accomplishment.

Your direct involvement in your children's projects isn't, in the long run, in their best interest regardless of the grades they make. In the long run, your support and encouragement will mean a lot more to their growth and development than an A on a project they really didn't do.

Q: We've already told our daughter, who's in the fourth grade, that she's to do her own projects. We will provide support, but we will not do them for her. The problem is that she will wait until the last minute before telling us that she has a project due, and then she expects us to panic along with her. What should we do in situations like that?

A: I'll tell you what we did with Amy. We did it once, and never had to do it again.

When Amy was in the fourth grade, she came to us one weekday afternoon and, looking very agitated, told us we *had* to drive her to the school supplies store, *right then*. We asked why the rush, and she told us that she had an important project due the next day. We then asked when the teacher had assigned the project, and Amy told us, sheepishly, "two weeks ago."

I looked at Willie, who shrugged her shoulders, as if to say, "tough."

So I said, "Amy, we're not going to take you to the store today."

She looked like someone stuck in the middle of a railroad trestle who'd just heard the sound of a train whistle. "But I'll get a bad grade if it's not in by tomorrow!" she screeched.

"You're probably right about that, Amy," I said.

She begged, she cried, she tried to make deals, persuade us to give her "one more chance," and so on. When that failed, she began to yell at us, tell us what horrible parents we were. When that failed, she ran to her room, sobbing.

The next day, we took her to get her supplies. She did the

project on her own, turned it in late, took a reduction in grade, and never waited until the last minute again.

Q: My daughter's kindergarten teacher recently started assigning homework. It really doesn't amount to much—just practice in forming letters and numbers, along with a page or two of coloring. Missy's problem is her dissatisfaction with her work. She doesn't make her numbers and letters well enough to suit herself and thinks her coloring is "ugly." Consequently, she winds up doing everything over three or four times when her first attempt was perfectly okay. The more help and encouragement I provide, the madder at herself she becomes. At times, she's made statements like "I'm dumb" and "I can't do anything!" Her teacher, however, sees none of this at school. In fact, she tells me Missy is one of the quickest learners in the class. How can I help her?

A: You can start by *not* helping her. The problem isn't Missy's work. It's her attitude toward herself, and by that I *don't* mean to imply that she has poor self-esteem or something along those lines.

Keep things in perspective. Missy is going through some fairly major changes right now. She's in school for the first time, she's learning new skills, she's trying to please you, she's trying to please the teacher, she's trying to please herself, and on top of all this, she has homework to contend with. Understandably, she feels a fair amount of pressure.

The way you manage the homework situation will be precedent-setting. In the final analysis, you want her to accept responsibility for her homework, set realistic goals for herself, and take pride in what she accomplishes. You certainly don't want her to become a neurotic little perfectionist at the age of five.

Two things are clear: First, you know she can do the work and do it well. The teacher's already assured you of that.

Second, she doesn't get bent out of shape about her work in school. We also know that the teacher, with twenty-five or so other kids in the class, is unable to give Missy the amount of attention you can. Ah-ha! So now we know that the less attention Missy gets, the less pressure she feels, the better her attitude is toward herself, and the more calmly and competently she works.

Now you know what to do! Stop giving her so much attention. In other words, stop helping her. The solution lies in implementing the ABC's of my homework management system, as described earlier in this chapter. Missy should do her homework in her room, she should receive your help only if she asks for it and then only if you decide she truly needs it, and she should be expected to finish her homework by a reasonable hour, say seven o'clock. Establishing a homework deadline will limit her obsessing and prevent homework from becoming a marathon.

If she complains about her performance, just say, "Do what you feel you need to do to get it right. Whatever you decide is fine with me. I love you and trust you to do your best." Don't, under any circumstances, try to persuade her that her work is fine when she's insisting it isn't. Just say a few encouraging words and excuse yourself from the room. This puts the "problem" in her lap, where she can decide what she wants to do about it.

Without intending to do so, Missy has manufactured this problem. There isn't a shred of evidence that it exists outside her imagination. In effect, it's a soap opera, and she's the producer. When you stop being the audience, it will quickly go off the air.

Q: Like Missy, our second-grader has become a perfectionist when it comes to his homework. He takes an inordinate amount of time forming and spacing his letters correctly and ends up erasing and starting over a lot because his first attempt doesn't suit him. Every Thursday night, I give him a practice spelling test, which is just about the only help he gets from me all week. I end up getting very frustrated with him because he takes so long to write each word. What should take ten minutes at most, takes thirty. His teacher says he was doing similar stuff at the beginning of the school year, but stopped when she put her foot down. When I put my foot down, however, all I get is a sore foot. Do you have a solution?

A: Yes, I do. In fact, I have not one, but two solutions. You can't beat that, now can you?

First solution: Make a rule that he can take as much time as he wants to write each word, but that you will only read words for fifteen minutes. When you start giving him his practice test, set a timer. When it rings, excuse yourself from the room, regardless of how many words there are left. As you leave, say, "I'm sure you can teach yourself the rest of these without me."

This forces him to make a crucial decision: Is it more important that he get through the list or that he write each word perfectly? This gives him an opportunity to experience and therefore begin to profit from the all-important "You Can't Have Your Cake and Eat It Too" principle. I'll just bet that the first few times you do this, the timer will ring before you've finished the list. I'll also bet that his spelling test grades won't suffer a bit.

There's an even better solution, however. I'm sure you'd agree that teaching your son *how* to study on his own is preferable to helping him study. At present, although your intentions can't be faulted, your "help" isn't really helping him develop good study skills. When parents help children with homework, especially when the help isn't necessary, children quickly become convinced they need the help. In other words, they become *dependent* upon it. When they become dependent upon the help, they begin doing things to perpetuate it, like taking thirty minutes to do something that should only take ten. Get it?

Ending the Hassle

As parents, our single most important job is that of teaching our children to stand on their own two feet. It's called self-sufficiency, and it's synonymous with self-esteem. The more children do for themselves, on their own, the more competent they feel. The more competent they feel, the more they want to do on their own, the more competent they act, and so on.

Second solution: Buy your son a cassette player/recorder and a blank tape and show him how to make his own spelling test—he reads a word into the recorder, pauses long enough to write the word, spells the word into the recorder, pauses again, reads the next word, and so on. Now his obsessing affects him and no one else. That forces him to decide whether he really wants to obsess or not.

I bet I know what decision he'll make.

Q: At the beginning of the year, our daughter's first-grade teacher sent a note home to all the parents requesting that they have the children read to them for thirty minutes every night. We can understand the reasoning behind the request, but carrying it out has been nothing but a hassle. Five minutes into the exercise and Lisa's had enough. From that point on, we must prod and scold to get her to finish. Meanwhile, her pronunciation gets increasingly sloppy and we get increasingly frustrated. All too often, the whole situation ends in tears. The real shame is that Lisa has always loved to have us read to her. Now, however, instead of being a joy, reading is fast becoming a drudge. Do you have any suggestions?

A: I sure am glad you asked, because yours is a tale familiar to thousands of other parents. All across America, children who once enjoyed having their parents read to them now dread reading to their parents. When the time comes, their reluctance emerges in the form of careless pronunciation, whining, and general dragging of feet (or eyeballs, as the case may be). Their parents might think they're just being lazy. But the problem lies not with the child but with the method.

Your daughter's teacher wants to accomplish a number of things with this nightly exercise. First, she wants the children to practice their reading skills at home. Second, she wants parents to become involved in their children's education. Third, she wants to keep parents abreast of their children's progress in reading. Fourth, she's probably hoping that the exercise is enjoyable for both parent and child, thereby increasing the child's motivation to read.

The teacher's purposes can't be faulted, but she's going about them in a most counterproductive manner. In the first place, even given a better method, thirty minutes is much too long a requirement. This age child's attention span for activities that require sitting in one spot, doing one thing, is simply not that long. Remember also what I said earlier in this chapter about *massed* versus *distributed* practice. As you've discovered, the point of diminishing returns is reached very early in this particular game.

Game? Not really, and that's the second, and biggest, problem. Simply stated, it's no fun! There's no play or give-and-take, only pressure to perform for thirty straight and tedious minutes. If there's a better way to make a child hate reading, I haven't heard of it.

Here, then, are my suggestions:

- Reduce the time to *ten* minutes. Better yet, agree to stop at a certain point, such as after one or two stories. You might tell the teacher of your intentions and explain to her your reasons, but if she objects, remember that you don't need her permission.
- Let your daughter choose at least some of what's to be read, even if it turns out to be something she's read many times before and knows by heart.
- Instead of having your daughter read to you the entire time, take turns reading to one another. You read a page, she reads a page, and so on. You can even alternate sentence by sentence.

Studies have shown that an early elementary school-age child's reading skills will improve simply as a result of being read to by an adult. When you read to her, hold the book so she can see it and follow along. This helps her learn to begin scanning more rapidly. Gradually, her reading speed will improve. Not only that, but she'll begin to see the whole word as a pattern, rather than the word as a potentially confusing sequence of phonetic elements, which can only be deciphered by memorizing equally confusing phonetic rules. Consequently, her "sight word" vocabulary will increase. Furthermore, by listening to you, she'll learn how to read with appropriate emphasis, which will enhance her comprehension of what she's reading.

Last, but by no means least, it will be enjoyable. And any reading exercise that fails to accomplish that isn't worth the time.

Q: We've been using your homework management system with our second-grade daughter for the last year, and with much success, we might add. She does her homework on her own, and asks us for help only occasionally. After finishing her work, however, she does ask us to check it. If we understand you correctly, that's okay, but we want to know what to do when we find mistakes. Should we point them out to her, or should we be less specific and let her figure them out for herself?

A: Yes, checking a child's work is perfectly okay, as long as the *child* initiates the request, which is what your daughter is doing. How you deal with mistakes is a judgment call, meaning there is no one answer to your question. Sometimes, it's more appropriate to refer specifically to the mistake, saying, "You might want to give this problem some more thought." Take note: This is different than saying, "You need to redo this." In other words, just put the ball in the child's court and let her decide what she wants to do with it.

At other times, it's more appropriate to say, "You've made several errors on this page. They look like careless mistakes to me. I'm sure you'll catch them yourself if you go over the assignment one more time."

In general, I'd lean toward the second option unless (a) the child was obviously tired or "burned out" on doing homework that evening; (b) the assignment was long, and going over it problem by problem would take a good deal of time (remember the pitfalls of mass practice); (c) the mistake was an isolated one and nothing would be gained by having the child find it on her own.

I'd also prefer the first option when, instead of pointing out an error, you're simply making a suggestion, as in, "This sentence is a bit long. What you're trying to say might be clearer if you made two sentences out of it, but that's up to you."

In the final analysis, the answer to your question is, "Use your common sense."

Q: Our fourteen-year-old daughter likes to do her homework with her radio on, turned to her favorite rock station. I don't see how she can do her best with that noise going in the background, but she not only says it doesn't bother her, she says she can't study without it. I've suggested that if she absolutely must have music on, at least make it classical or soft jazz. Forget it! That kind of music "bugs" her, she says. She maintains that as long as her grades are good (and they are) I have no right to interfere in how she does her homework. What do you think?

A: I agree completely with your daughter. When I was a teenager, I did my homework to the strains of Elvis, Buddy Holly, Dion and the Belmonts, and later, the Beatles and the Rolling Stones. Like you, my parents thought the music was a distraction. I always thought they objected more to my *selection* than to the idea of music in the background. Mozart would have been fine. After all, *he* was a genius. But they were convinced that Elvis's brains were in his pelvis and feared that too much exposure to his music would render me intellectually impotent. Little did they know how hard I wished that I, too, could be afflicted with Elvis's learning disability.

Actually, I think my grades were *better* because of rock 'n' roll. My English themes had rhythm, a backbeat. My math homework had symmetry. The music kicked me in the right side of my brain, unleashing my imagination, my sense of possibility, the power to see through the concrete to the abstract. A bop shu bop a bop bop shu bop yeah!

Remember that a kid's brain isn't as cluttered as an adult's. It's no sweat for a teenager to listen to rock 'n' roll with one part of the brain, do homework with another part, and still chew gum! After all, kids can do just about anything better and faster than adults. They learn new languages faster, they figure out Rubik's Cube faster, they can even keep a Hacky-Sack in the air longer than three seconds. Need I go on?

The older and more congested the brain gets, the more of a distraction rock music becomes to doing things such as homework. After age thirty or so, you have to start listening to classical or "new age" because that stuff stays in the background—it doesn't compete. Worse yet, we sometimes even talk ourselves into thinking we like it.

Several years ago, I was surprised to learn from a surgeon friend that operating rooms are equipped with expensive stereo systems and that most operations are performed to the tune of the surgeon's fave sounds. My friend's tastes ran to rhythm and blues from the fifties and sixties.

"Some of my best cuts," he once told me, "were made while listening to Otis Redding."

"Loud?" I asked.

"Is there any other way?" he answered with a grin.

I had this vision of doctors and nurses boogalooing around the O.R. to relieve the tension of the life-and-death matters they're dealing with. The point is that if doctors do heart transplants to Smokey Robinson and the Miracles, surely your daughter can do her homework to Led Zeppelin. At least I *hope* she's listening to stuff that good.

I agree with your daughter. As long as her grades are good, how she does her homework is none of your business. So, let the little girl rock!

Q: Almost every time my nine-year-old son, who's in the third grade, asks me to explain a homework problem to him, he gets upset either because he doesn't understand the explanation or because I don't do the problem the way his teacher wants it done. I find myself explaining over and over again, while he gets more and more upset. Finally, I reach the end of my rope and yell, which makes him cry, which makes me feel awful. Is there some secret to not losing one's patience in a situation like this?

A: There sure is! The secret is to stop trying to be so patient. It's your determination to help—no matter the cost—that's causing the problem.

Frustration prevents effective learning. Therefore, once your son begins getting frustrated because one of your explanations doesn't immediately register, he's rendered himself incapable of understanding. From that point, the more you try to explain, the more frustrated he's going to get, the less he's going to understand, and the more difficult it's going to be for you to teach him anything.

At the first sign of frustration, you should do yourself and your son a favor by getting up and calmly saying, "When you get upset, it becomes impossible for me to teach and impossible for you to learn. Perhaps I'm not the right person to be trying to explain this to you, anyway. I think you need to save this until tomorrow, when you can ask your teacher to explain it to you again." Then, disregarding any protests, walk away.

That gives him a choice. He can either regain his composure and politely ask you to explain it again, or he can try muddling through it on his own, or he can wait until the morrow and ask his teacher, as you suggested.

If he calms down and asks you for yet another explanation, but then begins getting upset again, separate yourself from the situation for the second, and last, time. Don't drag this ordeal out. Twice is enough.

Whether you can or can't successfully explain something to your son is not, after all, a test of your parenting ability. You aren't a teacher and it therefore isn't your job to make sure your child understands his lessons. That responsibility is shared by your son's teacher, whose job it is to communicate clearly, and your son, whose job it is to listen and ask appropriate questions.

Parents who get in the almost daily habit of re-explaining their children's homework lessons aren't doing their children's teachers any favors. The child who learns to rely on his parents for this sort of thing isn't likely to pay adequate attention in class. Why should he?

This isn't to say that parents shouldn't ever provide help of this sort, because in most instances, when a child asks for an explanation, the child should be given the benefit of the doubt. On the other hand, an effective consultant is the first to recognize when he's reached the limits of his expertise. He's the first to say, "I'm not the person you need for the job." That's not an admission of failure, it's an admission of fact. Furthermore, that admission doesn't diminish his credibility, it *enhances* it.

So take a page from the effective consultant's rulebook and give yourself permission to *not* accept an assignment. In this case, your "patience" is *not* a virtue.

Chapter Three

When to Motivate

More often than not, proper homework management is all it takes to turn an underachieving child around. At other times, it's not enough.

What if it isn't? What if you implement the ABC's of my homework management program, as described in the last chapter, and after a month or so of things getting worse, there's no sign they're *ever* going to get better? What if, in other words, the child seems hell-bent upon choosing failure?

Implementing my homework ABC's is an essential pre-requisite to solving *any* homework problem. In and of itself, however, the program will not completely solve *all* homework/ school performance problems. As I said in the last chapter, five out of ten "homework reluctant" children will begin turning themselves around—accepting responsibility for their home-work—within four weeks of exposure to the homework ABC's. For the other five, nothing much will have changed.

More often than not, a child who falls into this second category is suffering from prolonged lack of initiative. He's become so thoroughly dependent upon parental participation in his homework—and/or his life in general—that he's unable to muster what it's going to take to turn himself around, to accept responsibility for and solve his problems. If left to his own devices, he would, in fact, choose to fail. Not because he *wants* to fail, mind you, but because he simply doesn't know how to succeed. His parents, therefore, are going to have to take the bull by the horns and manage him toward making some correct decisions. I call it "jump-starting the child's motivational motor." Although his parents are going to have to get actively involved in the design and delivery of a motivational plan, there are ways for them to do so without becoming responsible for the child's problem.

An effective motivational plan must incorporate two key elements:

- First, the child's parents and teacher(s) must agree upon some means of *monitoring* the child's school performance. All concerned must take utmost care, however, not to cross the line between monitoring and hovering. For example, the teacher should *not* sign a list of homework assignments which the child prepares before leaving school and takes home to show his parents. As discussed in Chapter Two, strategies of this nature are *compensatory* in that they prevent the child from assuming complete responsibility for the problem. As such, they are forms of hovering. As I've already said (but cannot stress enough), it is impossible to compensate for a problem and correct it at the same time.
- Second, the child must be made *accountable* (responsible) for the problem. In other words, the child—and only the child—must shoulder both the emotional and practical consequences of the problem. In specific terms, if the child fails to do his homework, no one should get upset but the child, and no one should be inconvenienced but the child.

Motivating Christopher

As an example of how these two elements—monitoring and assigning responsibility—can be creatively joined, take the case of Christopher, an eight-year-old third grader. Christopher was obviously capable, but rarely finished an assignment in class. He spent most of the day "piddling," as his teacher put it—staring out the window, playing with his pencil, drawing, passing notes, and talking to other students. As a result, he carried both unfinished classwork *and* homework home with him. At least, he was *supposed* to bring his work

---

DAILY REPORT

Child: Christopher Jones

Date: _____

Teacher's Instructions: Christopher is responsible for bringing this report to you at the end of the day. If all three parts of the "Statement of Achievement" are true, sign your name in the space provided. If one or more parts of the statement are false, put an "X" instead of your signature. Comments are optional, but may be made in the space provided.

Statement of Achievement: Today, Christopher (1) completed his seatwork, (2) turned in his homework, and (3) everything was acceptable.

Signed _____
                          Mrs. Sally Smith

Teacher's Comments:

---

home. In fact, Christopher would not have brought everything (or maybe *anything*) home had his teacher not made sure before he left school that he had a list of his assignments as well as the books and workbooks needed to do them.

Beginning shortly after supper, he and his mother engaged in a world-class "Homework Hassle" until eight or nine o'clock every evening. She pushed, he pulled. She cared, he didn't. She went slowly crazy, he pretended not to notice.

Finally, on the verge of emotional meltdown, his mother asked for my advice. I began by having her implement my Homework ABC's. After several weeks, Christopher was as irresponsible and oblivious as ever. He was obviously in need of some creative management. With that in mind, I designed the "daily report card" shown above.

As the name implies, a daily report card monitors a child's school performance on a daily basis. In addition to a clear set of instructions for the teacher, a rating system of one sort or another, and a space for the teacher's comments, a daily report card incorporates, as its centerpiece, what I refer to as a "Statement of Achievement"—a concise definition of expectations.

Above all else, the Statement of Achievement should be attainable. It should reflect what the child is presently, and realistically, capable of accomplishing, not necessarily what people think the child is *eventually* capable of, or would have been capable of, had the problem never developed. A Statement of Achievement that is initially too difficult creates a "no win" situation for the child. In that case, the program will fail to motivate, and the problem will get *much* worse instead of better. Later, once the child is performing consistently at the level initially defined, the "ante" can be increased by making the Statement more difficult. Interestingly enough, however, I find that this is rarely necessary. Once a student gets "on track" with the program, his or her performance level almost always begins to exceed that defined by the Statement of Achievement.

Christopher was supplied with a folder full of daily report cards, which he kept in his desk at school. At the end of the school day, he removed one from the folder and took it up to his teacher. If his performance for that day matched the goals set forth in the Statement of Achievement, she signed her name. If not, she put a large "X" in place of her signature. Note that it was an "all or nothing" proposition: The Statement had to be completely true in order for Christopher to earn his teacher's signature. If even one part of the Statement was false, he received an "X."

The daily report card provided the monitoring needed. Now, the accountability—Christopher brought the report home and immediately turned it over to his mother. If he had earned his teacher's signature, he was able to go outside, have a friend over, and watch his normal allotment of television. In other words, Christopher was able to enjoy his normal, everyday standard of living (consisting of privileges, not rewards). If the report came home with an "X" instead of a signature, then

Christopher's standard of living (going outside, having friends over, watching television) for the day was taken away. If the report didn't come home at all, Christopher still lost his standard of living, but he also had to go to his room after supper and stay there until his bedtime, which came one hour early. No excuses were accepted for no report. This additional penalty for no report made it less likely that Christopher would "lose" those that were unflattering.

On days when Christopher earned his teacher's signature, a star was put in that day's box in the Star Chart shown on the next page, which was magnetized to the refrigerator. If Christopher was absent from school for a legitimate reason (illness, vacation day), he earned a star automatically. At the end of the week, the total number of stars determined Christopher's privileges for Saturday and Sunday, as follows:

Less than Three Stars = Christopher is on full restriction, meaning he cannot go outside, cannot have a friend over, cannot watch television, and goes to bed early.

Three Stars = In addition to the above, Christopher can stay up until his regular bedtime on Saturday and Sunday nights and can watch one hour of television each day.

Four Stars = In addition to the above, Christopher can go outside on Sunday and can watch two hours of television (his usual allotment) each weekend day.

Five Stars = Christopher can go outside on Saturday and can have a friend over on both days (even to spend the night).

This meant that on any given day of the week, Christopher was working not only for that day's privileges, but Saturday's and Sunday's as well. This combination of short- and longer-term incentives works much better than short-term incentives alone, and is absolutely necessary for those kids that attend after-school care and don't get home until nearly six o'clock, since most of their "free time" may already be gone.

Christopher's Star Chart

week begins _____

MON	TUE	WED	THU	FRI	TOTAL

Note that it was Christopher's responsibility to remember to take the report to his teacher at the end of the day. It was *not* her responsibility to remember for him. And it was Christopher's responsibility to get the report home. If it didn't get there, no one went looking for it.

The teacher's job was simply to determine, at the end of every day, whether Christopher had or had not met the goals set forth in the Statement of Achievement. She took a few minutes to look over his work to make sure it was all there and that he'd done a reasonably good job with it. Then she made her mark.

All Christopher's parents had to do was enforce the rules. If Christopher came home without a signature, they didn't ask for an explanation. Nor did they get mad or give him a lecture. They simply kept him inside, kept him away from the television, and if a friend came calling, sent the friend away. They were calm, cool, and collected, and in so doing, *they let the problem be Christopher's.*

Christopher tested the system for two weeks. At first, he

acted like he didn't care whether he got a signature or not. Then he tried arguing with his teacher when she wouldn't give him a signature. When that didn't work, he begged, promising, "I'll do better tomorrow!" At home, he pleaded for "just one more chance." When pleading didn't work, he cried and threatened to run away from home. He came home without the report a few times, saying that he left it at school, or lost it, or the school bully took it away, or it blew out the window of the bus, but always insisting, "I got a signature from my teacher! Really!" His parents listened, shrugged their shoulders, and said, "That's too bad, Christopher. We hope you manage to get your report home tomorrow."

When Christopher finally found out that the problem belonged to him, and him alone, and that no one was going to bail him out of whatever mess he made for himself, he began bringing home signatures. At first, just a few. Then, slowly but surely, he began bringing home more and more until he was bringing a signature home nearly every day.

Once Christopher was on the right track, we kept the program going for another three months, just to make sure. Then, his parents sat down with him and said, "Christopher, we're very proud of the progress you've made in school. You're doing the work assigned in class, doing your homework on your own, and your grades have gotten better and better. We've decided that if you don't want to carry the daily report any longer, you don't have to. But, if you decide not to, we still expect good work in school. If you start having the same old problems, we'll have to start the daily reports again."

Christopher said, "I won't need 'em again." And he was right!

Civilizing Derek

Sometimes, a child's academic difficulties are simply a by-product of classroom behavior problems. By resolving the behavior problems, you resolve the academic problems as well. As

the following story—about a second-grade boy named Derek—
illustrates, daily reports can be modified for this purpose.

Derek was your basic generic hellion. I met him and his
parents the summer between his first- and second-grade years.
They had been referred to me by the school counselor, who
described him as "The Great Pretender." In the company of
adults, and particularly if he was the center of attention, Derek
was the "perfect" kid—considerate, mannerly, polite. Watching him work a crowd of big people, no one would have
dreamed that Derek was the same kid about whom his first
grade teacher had said . . .

". . . he seems to lack knowledge of how to relate to other
children his age. He hits, bites, and kicks other children
and will then deny having done so even when observed 'in
the act' by an adult. Just the other day, he pummeled a child
for accidentally bumping into him in line. A week ago, he
punched a little girl in the stomach and knocked the breath
out of her. In the classroom, he talks out of turn, shouts out
the answers to questions without raising his hand, wanders
around the room when he should be working, and manages
to distract and disrupt those around him. Although he's
smart and more than capable, he spends so much time
misbehaving that he ends up not finishing most of the work
he's supposed to do in class. One-on-one, however, he's a
wonderful little person."

According to his parents, Derek had been aggressive toward other children even as a toddler. He'd been an only child
until age five, when a new brother came into the family. The
older the little brother became, the more jealousy Derek displayed.

His parents had all but given up on trying to get him to do
even so much as pick up after himself around the house. As his
mother put it, "It's easier to do it myself than go through the
hassle of trying to get him to do anything." He tested limits
constantly, and his parents had fallen into a fairly consistent

pattern of compromising with and giving in to him in order to maintain a tentative peace.

Derek would do anything to be the center of attention. He was the master of "uproar." He started the day by refusing to get out of bed and ended it by refusing to go to bed. In between, he was demanding, disruptive, and disrespectful.

After careful consideration of the presenting symptoms, I diagnosed Derek a "mess." At the end of their second visit, his parents asked me why he acted the way he did. I suppose they were looking for some highbrow psychological analysis along the lines of (German accent, please), "Derek's expressions of hostility are symptomatic of significant loss of self-esteem traceable to unresolved jealousies and feelings of parental betrayal related to the birth of his male sibling, blah, blah, blah." Instead, I took a deep breath and told them the truth: "I don't really know."

I let the shock sink in for a moment or two, then said, "I hate to disappoint you folks, but if you want me to explain Derek's behavior, I can't. I can speculate—and impressively so, I assure you—but explanations often tend to confound more than they clarify. If we say that his problems stem from jealousy toward his brother, where do we go from there? Can you unbirth your second child? If jealousy is the problem, then it would seem logical to give Derek more attention. But we already know that the more attention he gets, the more he wants, and the worse his behavior becomes.

"This I do know: Derek's his own worst enemy. He dislikes himself for behaving the way he does, but hasn't the faintest notion of how to begin behaving better. That's where we come in. The adults in his life have to lead him out of the labyrinth. And we will!"

Just before the start of the new school year, I held a conference with the guidance counselor and second-grade teacher. Upon review, we broke the overall problem down into the five most troublesome behaviors. They were (in no particular order):

   1. Teasing other children (verbal aggression);
   2. Hurting other children (physical aggression);
   3. Arguing with adults (denying obvious wrong-doing);
   4. Talking out of turn or during instruction (blurting);
   5. Getting out of his seat without permission (wandering).

Those five behaviors—called *target behaviors*—were listed on an index card. Soon thereafter, the teacher and guidance counselor went over them with Derek, giving examples of each. The list was then taped to the wall behind the teacher's desk.

Every day, Derek brought the daily report card shown below to school and, before the first bell, gave it to his teacher, who put it on her desk. Every time Derek displayed a target behavior, she called it to his attention, walked to her desk, crossed off the highest remaining block (beginning with block 6), and resumed whatever she was doing. Every target behavior resulted in the loss of the next highest block. If a target behavior or behaviors occurred on the playground or in the cafeteria, Derek's teacher crossed off a block (or blocks) when she returned to the classroom.

DAILY REPORT

For: Derek   **Date:**

6	5	4
3 **Play Outside** **Have a Friend Over**	**2** **Watch Television**	**1** **Your Normal** **Bedtime**

Teacher: _____   **Comments**
                                              on back

At the end of the school day, the teacher signed the card, put whatever comments she felt like making on the back, and handed it to Derek, who took it home and gave it to his mother. The first three blocks (6, 5, 4) were "free," meaning that Derek incurred no consequences as a result of losing them. They constituted his "margin of error" for the day. Loss of blocks 3, 2 or 1, however, meant the loss of the privileges associated with them at home. For example, if Derek lost block 3 at school, then he was not allowed to play outside or have a friend over after school. If he lost block 2, he couldn't watch television at home. If he lost block 1, he went to bed one hour early. If Derek arrived at home sans card, it was treated as if he'd lost all of his blocks at school, and he was confined to his room until bedtime. No excuses or explanations were accepted.

The program built a bridge of communication between Derek's teacher and his parents. It also meant that the consequences of his misbehavior at school followed him home. The choice presented to Derek was simple and clear: Control yourself at school and you can enjoy your standard of living at home. Lose control and you begin losing your standard of living as well.

In mid-October, I held a conference with the teacher. She described him as "completely different" from the child described to her by the first-grade teacher. Although he'd had some problems the first few weeks of the new school year, he straightened himself out quickly. The more his behavior improved, the more attention he paid to his work. On his first report card, the teacher remarked that Derek was "making excellent progress both academically and socially."

"I am very pleased," she wrote, "with his conduct and his eagerness to express himself properly."

The teacher and I talked again in November. "There's been a marked improvement just since the last time we spoke," she said. "He's really a nice little boy."

She went on to tell me that he'd become quite popular with the other children, and was among the first chosen for team play at recess.

At home, his parents reported that not only was he more cooperative and respectful, but he was also playing patiently and gently with his little brother and even reading to him.

We suspended the program in March, informing Derek that he'd "graduated," but reserving the option of starting it back up again if his behavior began to deteriorate, which it never did.

High School Harry

For several reasons, it would be laughable to even attempt a daily report in a junior high or high school setting: First, because work isn't always assigned on a daily basis, teachers would frequently have no concrete means of assessing the student's performance. Second, if—as is often the case in junior and senior high school—there was no "free time" during class, the rating would have to be obtained after the bell, which might make the student late for his next class, thus jeopardizing his rating there. Third, junior high/high school teachers themselves have little, if any, time between classes, and ratings assigned under pressure are generally not accurate reflections of student achievement.

The solution is to use a *weekly* monitoring system whereby the student carries a report from teacher to teacher on Friday or the last day of the school week, whichever the case may be. The weekly report I recommend for use with High School Harrys (and Harriets) is shown below.

Note that the Statement of Achievement is cumulative, in that the teacher is being asked to rate how well the student has performed *to date* in the current grading period. In other words, the first weekly report of the grading period only covers the student's performance during that week. The second weekly report, however, covers the student's performance during weeks one and two. Therefore, any deficiencies incurred during week one which are not corrected prior to the second Friday would also show up on the second report. The third weekly report would cover weeks one, two, and three, and so on.

WEEKLY REPORT

Student's Name: _____

For Week Ending: _____

Instructions to Teachers: _____ will bring this report to you on Friday of every week. Please take the time to respond to the "Statement of Achievement" by circling either "Yes" or "No" and signing your name in the space provided. **Please use ink. Note that both parts of the "Statement of Achievement" must be true in order for _____ to earn a rating of "Yes" for the week.** Comments are optional, but please feel free to use the space at the bottom for any you feel are appropriate. Thank you.

Statement of Achievement: Up until this point in the current grading period, _____ **(1)** is passing my class with a grade of "C" or better, and **(2)** he/she is not missing any assignments.

Subject	Teacher	Rating	Signature
Math	Adams	Yes No	_____
Lang. Arts	Smith	Yes No	_____
Soc. Studies	Jones	Yes No	_____
Health	Collins	Yes No	_____
Env. Science	Johnson	Yes No	_____
P.E.	King	Yes No	_____

Comments:

The fact that deficiencies "follow" the student in this manner means that they must be resolved in order to obtain satisfactory ratings. If the report was not cumulative, a student could conceivably "get away" with putting forth satisfactory effort on a selective basis, whereas a cumulative report requires consistently good performance throughout the grading period.

In the example above, the student is required to maintain a "C" average in every subject. The initial standard should be no higher than this, even if the student is capable of better grades. As the youngster becomes more responsible, the Statement of Achievement can be changed to reflect higher performance standards. Even if the student is capable of straight "A's," however, the Statement should never require more than a "B" in every subject. (By the way, nonacademic subjects, like band and physical education, are optional and should only be included in the report if the child has been having difficulties in them or those teachers want to participate in the program. For that matter, the report can target only those subjects in which the youngster has had previous difficulty.)

Also note that teachers are asked to use ink when filling out the report. This shouldn't require explanation. I also recommend that parents obtain a sample signature from each teacher prior to the start-up of the system. Kids are smart, but teenagers are *clever*. If you don't get at least a step ahead of them, and stay there, you'll find yourself reacting—after the fact—to one mischievously inventive maneuver after another.

Finally, the report is simple, which lessens the time it takes a teacher to fill it out. The more complex the report, the greater the chance that teachers will simply "rubber stamp" it from week to week.

Before initiating a weekly report, the student's parents should meet with all of the participating teachers as a group. This meeting can be arranged through either the guidance counselor or principal, and at least one, if not both of them, should attend. The importance of this preliminary step cannot be stressed enough. Remember that the report is simply a vehicle for communication. A face-to-face conference is the most effective way of setting the ball in motion as well as the best way of preventing misunderstandings.

The preliminary conference sets the stage and puts everyone on the same "wavelength." Everyone hears the same explanation and gets a chance to ask questions. The conference gives teachers a chance to have some input into such things as the design of the report, the actual wording of the Statement of Achievement, and when and how the student is to present the report to them. It goes without saying that the more active a role they have in the planning process, the greater the chances of success become. Also, the parents' presence at the conference is a demonstration of their commitment to the goals of the program. It forms the basis for continued communication and creates a sense of "teamwork" that cannot be established as effectively using any other means.

Last, but not least, there's the matter of accountability. For a teacher to say, "Yes, I'll do this," in front of a group that includes several of his or her peers as well as a guidance counselor and/or the principal binds that teacher's participation in the program and makes later attempts to drop out of or sabotage the program far less likely.

The initial conference should not be dismissed without first scheduling a follow-up. This second meeting of the minds should take place midway through the grading period. (As I discuss later, it's generally best to begin a weekly report program at the start of a new grading period.) This gives everyone enough time to develop a working "feel" for the program and identify problems that may require group discussion. The student's parents and each teacher should come prepared to make a progress report. The primary purpose, however, of this second meeting is to make whatever adjustments in the design, logistics, or administration of the program that might be necessary. Future follow-up conferences should be held no less frequently than once per grading period, or more often if needed.

One of the most important topics to cover at the initial conference is the rules of the program, of which there are four:

RULE 1: *The student is completely responsible for remembering to take a report to school every Friday (or the last day of the school week).*

This simply means that parents are not to ask, "Are you remembering to take your report?" before the youngster leaves for school on Friday. How the student wants to handle this is his/her business. It doesn't take long for most of them to figure out that the simplest way to avoid problems is to keep a supply of reports in their lockers at school or in their notebooks. Some students, after forgetting to bring a report from home, have improvised one at school. As long as the improvisation contains the necessary information in clear form, it's acceptable.

RULE 2: *The student is responsible for obtaining a rating and a signature from each of his/her teachers every Friday (or the last day of the school week). The student is to arrange with each teacher a convenient time to obtain this information.*

In other words, a teacher is *not* to chase the student down after class on Friday if he/she has "forgotten" to obtain a rating. Although each teacher is going to have personal preferences concerning how this is accomplished, most teachers have the student present the report at the beginning of class on Friday, which gives them the flexibility of the entire period to complete it. Some teachers may prefer that the student return after school on Friday to obtain the rating. Students tend to complain that this inconveniences them with respect to after-school plans they might have made, to which I suggest the following reply: "No one is inconveniencing you. You have inconvenienced yourself though your own lack of responsibility. Put your priorities in order and you will be inconvenienced no longer."

RULE 3: *The student is responsible for bringing the report home every Friday afternoon and showing it to his/her parents as soon as one of them arrives home. No excuses are accepted if the student fails to either bring the report home or obtain a rating/signature from one or more teachers. Coming home with no report is equivalent to having a "NO" rating from every teacher. A rating without a signature, or a signature without a rating, counts as a "NO" rating.*

Unless permission has been obtained in advance, the student is to come directly home from school on Friday, report in hand. When it says that "No excuses are accepted," it means exactly that. None. Zero. Zilch. The student can opt to ask the teacher or teachers to complete the report the following Monday, but they are under no obligation to do so. If they agree to this, however, and if the ratings are such that no restriction would have resulted, then privileges are reinstated for the remainder of the week, at which time another report is due.

RULE 4: *Under no circumstances can a substitute teacher sign the report. If a teacher is absent on Friday, making it impossible for the student to obtain that teacher's rating, the student must obtain a note from either the counselor, principal, or assistant principal stating that the teacher was, in fact, absent during the period in question. The note should be written in the "Comments" section of the report and must be signed in order to be valid. If a teacher is absent, and the student obtains the required note, that teacher's rating is counted as a "YES".*

The first weekly report system I designed was for a tenth-grader whose grades had been in a steady state of decline for several years. The first Friday's report came in with three "NO" ratings, which meant the youngster was placed on complete restriction for the week (see Rule 5). The next report contained "YES" ratings from every teacher, but three of those ratings—and, coincidentally, the same three that had been "NO's" the previous week—were from substitute teachers. My crap detector went off like an air-raid siren. I called the school and discovered, sure enough, there had been no substitute teachers. Realizing she hadn't done what she needed to turn the "NO's" to "YES's," the student had sympathetic friends sign the names of three fictitious "substitutes." Very clever, these modern teenagers. Ha! To tell the truth, I would have tried the same thing under similar circumstances. Kids haven't changed much in twenty-five years.

RULE 5: *The student's report can contain one "NO" rating without penalty. However, if the student obtains a "NO" rating in the same subject two weeks in a row, he/she is on complete restriction (no special events, no television, no telephone calls made or received, no socializing with friends outside of school) until such time as the rating in that subject becomes a "YES."*

RULE 6: *Two "NO" ratings in the same week result in full restriction until the following Friday. At that time, if both "NO" ratings have become "YES" ratings, the student is no longer on restriction (unless he/she has incurred two new "NO" ratings). If one or both of the "NO" ratings remain unchanged, then RULE 5 applies.*

As you can see, the consequences are quite simple. The student either retains (as opposed to *earns*) privileges or doesn't. Some parents and teachers have raised concerns about the built-in allowance involving one, and only one, "NO" rating. They ask, "Doesn't that mean that the student can get away with being lax in a different subject each week?" I answer, "Theoretically, that's possible, but it would require more energy to keep up with such a complex scheme than it would to just do the work required in each subject, and if a student's smart enough to figure it out, he's also smart enough to figure out what a waste of time it is."

Once the student's parents have held a joint conference with the necessary teachers, once the report itself has been designed and printed and the logistics of the program have been worked out, the program is ready for lift-off.

At this point, the student is informed of the plans that have been made in his/her behalf (don't expect expressions of appreciation), given a supply of reports, and told of the need to make plans with each teacher concerning how the report is to be handled every Friday. Encourage the student to make those plans before the first Friday of the program, but start the program on time regardless. If the student brings the report to a teacher who refuses to sign it, saying, "Sorry, but you should have made arrangements with me earlier in the week," it's the student's problem, as it should be.

Remember that the entire point of a program of this nature is to assign responsibility to the child—and *only* the child—for his/her school performance. The rules are designed to do just that. *The child* is responsible for arranging with each teacher an appropriate/convenient time for obtaining his/her rating and signature. *The child* is responsible for remembering to take a report to school on Friday of every week. *The child* is responsible for remembering to take the report from teacher to teacher. *The child* is responsible for making sure each teacher uses ink. *The child* is responsible for obtaining the necessary note if there's a substitute. *The child* is responsible for bringing the card home. The teachers do no more than check their gradebooks once a week, give their ratings, and sign the report. The parents do no more than enforce the consequences of the program.

The program can be started anytime; however, if the student is so far behind the "eight-ball" in certain subjects that he or she can't possibly obtain satisfactory ratings from those teachers, then the start-up of the program should coincide with the start of a new grading period. This effectively wipes the slate clean and gives the student a fair shot at success from the very beginning.

Typically, it takes a student about three weeks to get "on track" and begin bringing home consistently satisfactory reports. Once the student is bringing home good reports from one week to the next, parents should continue to run the program for an additional eight weeks, at the very least. This "nails down" the improvement and prevents a relapse. At that point, if everything is going well, then the program can be discontinued with the understanding that it will be reactivated should problems again begin to develop.

I've had some people ask, "What's the difference between this program and just putting the kid on restriction until the next report card comes in?"

The answer is that putting a child on long-term restriction is usually counterproductive. A child who can't see the "light at the end of the tunnel" is likely to just say, "Oh, what the heck!" and give up. As the next story illustrates, this isn't always the case; nonetheless, long-term restrictions (more than two weeks) should be used with caution and conservatism.

A Few Words about Reality

Notice that rewards were not used to entice satisfactory performance out of Christopher and High School Harry. Why? Because rewards don't work to motivate those that aren't already well-motivated, that's why. Oh, they'll work for a while, but after an underachieving child saturates on whatever reward is being offered, the reward loses its "motivational" value. At that point, in order to renew the child's performance, the reward must be increased. That could go on forever.

The nature of a reward-based system means that the child is not having to accept responsibility for the problem. His parents are continuing to accept responsibility every time they dig down into their pockets for the cash needed to keep the rewards coming. Meanwhile, instead of learning that good performance—doing one's best—is its own best reward, the child is learning that good performance is only worth it if there's something in it for him. He's learning to be stingy enough about good performance to keep the offers coming, and to dish out just enough good performance to keep cashing in on them. I don't mean to say that children shouldn't be praised for their accomplishments, because they should be. Realize, however, that praise doesn't *create* motivation, it simply helps maintain it.

A system that uses privileges instead of rewards is far more effective because it's reality-based. In other words, it's consistent with the way the world works. Let's say you begin misbehaving in your job—you start coming in late for work, you take too many breaks, and you're consistently behind schedule with the work you're supposed to do. Does your supervisor finally get fed up enough with you to say, "Okay, okay! I'll tell you what: If you'll do the job you're supposed to do this week, and do it well, I'll take you out and buy you a new car!"

Hardly. He is more likely to take you into his office and say, "I can no longer tolerate your misbehavior. As a result, I'm writing you up. If you continue to misbehave, I'll have no choice but to terminate you."

In other words, he *threatens your standard of living*. Everyone is motivated to protect and improve their standard of living. Once you get accustomed to a certain standard, you don't want to lose it. Children are the same as everyone else. They are also motivated to protect and improve their standards of living. Adults measure their standards in terms of purchasing power; children measure theirs in terms of privilege—how often they can go outside, how far they can venture unsupervised, how often friends can come over, how much television they can watch, and how late they can stay up.

Threatening a child's standard of living is central to what I call *The Agony Principle*. It is a simple statement of accountability that proposes that *parents should never agonize over a child's behavior if the child is perfectly capable of agonizing over it himself.* The actual threat—which isn't really a threat, but a promise—is an example of what I refer to as *The Godfather Principle*. Borrowed from the late Sicilian philosopher Don Corleone, it states that in order to motivate someone to do what he or she is supposed to do, you must "make 'em an offer they can't refuse."

For comic relief, I make it sound sinister, but it's really not. It's simply the way the real world works. And if it's the job of big people to equip children with the skills they will need to successfully negotiate the real world, then it's our job to describe that world to them in accurate terms.

The Story of Eric: Part One

As a further example of how the Agony and Godfather Principles work, take the true story of a fifth-grade boy named Eric. Eric Rosemond. Interesting coincidence, don't you think?

About a month into the school year, one of Eric's teachers called his parents and alerted them to the fact that Eric was, well, goofing off, although the teacher didn't put it quite that bluntly.

"Eric's a great kid," she said, "and certainly capable of doing excellent work, but he prefers to socialize rather than use his time wisely. The problem is that he's already in danger of failing two or three subjects."

The teacher suggested that Eric start writing his homework assignments in a notebook before leaving school.

"I'll make sure he's written his assignments down correctly," she said, "and you can follow up at home by checking to make sure he's done all his work."

Eric's parents didn't like that idea. "We appreciate your suggestion, and agree that it would be a good idea for Eric to write down his assignments before leaving school," said Eric's father, "but to tell you the truth, his mother and I don't want to check behind him concerning his homework. We feel that Eric should accept that responsibility on his own."

After a pause, the teacher said, "But how is he going to learn unless we help him?" She sounded a bit defensive. Eric's father could tell that she was holding her irritation in check.

"We think he'll learn to be responsible once he discovers that the consequences of being irresponsible aren't worth it," Mr. Rosemond replied. "For example, we expect you to give him *exactly* the grades he earns. If you'll take care of consequences at school, we'll take care of consequences at home. What do you think?"

The teacher said she thought her idea was better, but added, "He's your son."

That evening, his parents told Eric about the teacher's call. After recounting the discussion, Eric's father said, "We expect you to solve this problem, Eric. If you don't, then your mother and I will have no choice but to take a more active role in this matter. For the time being, however, your performance in school is your business, and we promise not to interfere."

Several weeks later, Eric brought home three "D's" on his report card. At least two of them were, in all likelihood, gifts from a teacher who couldn't bear to give "F's" to a child whose parents were so "irresponsible." His parents had a talk with him. They told him that, although they didn't expect straight "A's," they wouldn't—under any circumstances—accept "D's" or "F's."

Eric's father said, "One of us will go to the school in four weeks and talk with your teacher. If she tells us that you have completely solved this problem, you will be allowed to leave the house. If not, you'll be confined another four weeks."

Eric's eyes grew wide and panicky, his lower jaw dropped open, and a look of complete incredulity spread over his face.

"Wha-a-a-t?!?!" he exclaimed.

"That's right, Eric," his father said. "For the next month, you'll be confined to the house after school and on weekends. You won't be allowed to have friends over or talk on the phone. After supper, you'll go to your room—where there will be no stereo—and remain there until bedtime. The good news is we promise that during the next four weeks we will not so much as even ask you if you have homework. The ball is completely in your court. Like I said, everything depends on that conference with the teacher four weeks from now."

"Well, uh, Dad," Eric asked, "could you maybe go back to the school in two weeks instead of four?"

"Nope. Once every four weeks is already too often for us to be making trips to the school because of problems you should never have created in the first place, so that's the best offer you're going to get."

For the next month, Eric's parents followed through exactly as promised. During that time, they never once asked him if he had homework, never once checked to see whether he was doing homework, never once called the teacher. They left him totally on his own, to be totally responsible for the problem and its solution.

When they went to see Eric's teacher, she gave them an excellent report.

"I don't know what you did, but Eric's made a complete turn-around," she said, "he's turning in all of his homework, paying attention in class, and his test grades have been excellent."

"We didn't do much of anything," Eric's father said. "Just gave him a little time to think, and something to think about, that's all."

The Story of Eric: Part Two

Halfway through his sophomore year in high school, Eric turned sixteen and, shortly thereafter, obtained his driver's license. No longer dependent on us or anyone else for transportation, he began spending less time at home, which is typical and perfectly understandable. It became apparent to us, however, that he wasn't devoting sufficient time to his studies. When we expressed concern, he gave us the standard song and dance about high school being harder, to which we replied, "Yes, we know. And college is harder still, and the real world is harder than that, so it's time you started working harder, don't you agree?"

Then he said he didn't know if he could bring up his grade in one subject because that teacher didn't like him, to which we replied, "Success in life consists of equal parts potential, perseverance, and personality, kid. In other words, getting along with your teachers is every bit as important as knowing the subject matter. You need to straighten out whatever problems you've created in your relationship with that teacher, because that excuse simply doesn't fly around here."

Placed squarely in checkmate, Eric had no choice but to say, "I'll do better."

But he didn't. A few weeks later, midterm reports came out and, sure enough, his grades had slipped.

"Don't worry," he said, "I'll bring them back up before the end of the grading period."

We believed him, but just to make sure, we borrowed a lesson from the Godfather and made Eric an offer he couldn't refuse.

Every Friday, he was required to carry the form shown below from class to class and obtain from each of his academic teachers a statement of his current grade average in that subject. As you see, each teacher filled in Eric's numerical grade average and signed his/her name. By the way, the statement was not acceptable unless both the grade and signature were in

---

WEEKLY REPORT
Eric

Teachers' Instructions: Eric is responsible for bringing this report to you at the end of class on Friday or the last day of the school week. Please average his grades TO THIS POINT IN THE GRADING PERIOD and put his grade average in the space provided next to your subject and sign your name. PLEASE USE INK! Comments are optional, but may be added at the bottom. Thank you.

Subject	Teacher	Current Grade Average	Teacher's Signature
English	Richmond	_____	_____
Algebra	Wang	_____	_____
World Hist.	Tuchman	_____	_____
Chemistry	Peters	_____	_____
Civics	Kennedy	_____	_____

Comments:

---

ink. If he came home without a grade from a teacher, it would be averaged in as a zero.

We decided that Eric's grades had to average 85 or above and no single grade could be below 77, which was the cut-off between "C" and "D." If either criterion was not met, Eric would not be able to use the car until the following Friday, and then only if he had corrected the problem and brought home an acceptable daily report. When I was sixteen, nothing was more important to me than being able to drive. I was confident that times hadn't changed.

The first week's reports came in below 85, and Eric pleaded for us to give him one more chance. We said, "You have another chance next Friday. Meanwhile, you don't drive." That was the first and last week he failed to earn driving privileges.

We required the reports for about eight weeks, then suspended them with the option of reinstatement if problems developed again. In the meantime, his grades came steadily back up to pre-driver's license levels.

The program made Eric responsible for his own freedom, so we weren't the "bad guys." Furthermore, because he could see light at the end of the tunnel from one week to the next, the system was far more motivating than long-term restriction of the nebulous "until your grades improve" variety.

Thank you, Don Corleone.

Before We Go Any Further . . .

Let's review what I've said thus far:

First, I said that the Homework ABC's set forth in Chapter Two, if implemented early enough, should prevent homework problems from ever developing.

Second, that five out of ten children with already-developed homework problems, after three or four week's exposure to the Homework ABC's, will begin turning around and accepting responsibility for their school performance.

Third, that of the other five children who don't show any improvement in response to the Homework ABC's, two or three will begin turning around after being put on a motivational program of one sort or another.

That still leaves two or three children. My experience tells me that those are kids who need, in addition to motivational management, special help of one sort or another. In order to determine just what kind of help is needed, you're going to need to gather and process some important information, and you may need professional assistance in doing so.

Evaluating Your Child's Abilities and Skills

Before deciding upon a course of action for a child who doesn't respond to a motivational program of the sort described in the previous chapter, there are three basic questions that must be answered:

First, "What achievement level is reasonable to expect of the child?" In other words, "What is the child's overall level of ability?"

Second, "Are the child's actual skills in reading, language arts, and math on a par with his/her ability level?"

Third, "Are the child's skills such that he/she is presently capable of doing grade-level work in school?"

These important questions can often be answered by looking over previous report cards, examining the child's performance on standardized achievement tests such as the Iowa Test of Basic Skills (ITBS) or the California Achievement Test (CAT), and talking with the child's teachers, past and present. This initial inquiry should render a good working "picture" of the child, and from that you can usually make a fairly accurate determination of the child's level of ability as well as his/her current level of academic proficiency and standing relative to grade level.

In some cases, this information is sufficient to begin making some strategic decisions, but if this initial investigation generates more questions than it answers, then a more formal evaluation is called for. This is especially the case if . . .

- the academic record is extremely inconsistent;
- the child's history has been complicated by developmental delays or chronic medical problems of one sort or another;
- the child has been having the same or similar academic problems for more than a year;
- the child began having problems almost from "day one" of entering school;
- academic performance is far below what everyone, and the evidence, says the child is capable of doing;
- academic performance is below grade level;
- there is evidence of learning difficulties, including evidence of a learning disability (see Chapter Four) and/or attention deficit disorder (see Chapter Six);
- grades and/or standardized test scores have deteriorated or fluctuated markedly from one year to the next.

If even one of these is true of your child, then you should obtain a formal assessment through a child or educational psychologist. That formal assessment will include, as its centerpiece, an evaluation of general aptitudes and abilities, accomplished with what is popularly known as an "IQ" test. At present, the two most widely used are the Wechsler Intelligence Scale for Children-Revised (WISC-R) and the Stanford-Binet Intelligence Scale. In addition, two or three tests of academic achievement will be given to determine the child's current achievement levels in reading (word recognition), reading comprehension, language arts (spelling and written expression), and math. In most cases, the psychologist will also assess the child's perceptual-motor functioning (eye-hand coordination).

It's important for parents to know that a so-called "IQ" test does *not* determine how smart a child is. The concept of intelligence includes consideration of an individual's creative abilities, social skills, athletic abilities, and even self-concept, none of which are evaluated by either the WISC-R or the Stanford-Binet.

These tests, or *scales*, as they are more accurately called, sample the child's abilities in only *two* areas of intelligence—verbal knowledge/reasoning and nonverbal reasoning—both of which, however, are highly correlated with school achievement. The child's performance on the particular scale being used yields information that is helpful in two key ways. First, by sampling the child's abilities, it answers the first of our three questions: "What achievement level is reasonable to expect of the child?" For example, a child who performs consistently within the average range on a test of general abilities shouldn't be expected to perform above grade level in school, while scores that occupy the significantly above average range tell us that, in all likelihood, the child is capable of being at least a strong "B" student with minimal effort. Second, the child's performance profile can help in the detection and diagnosis of specific learning problems, such as learning disabilities and attention deficit disorder.

Some parents, when I·suggest that an evaluation of this sort is in order, say, "We already know he can do the work."

"And *how* do you know?" I'll ask.

"Because whenever we sit down and go over the work with him, he shows us he can do it."

I hardly have the heart to tell these folks that they're comparing apples to oranges, that the true measure of a child's ability level is not what he can produce when someone sits down one-on-one and coaxes answers out of him. The true measure is what the child can produce independently.

Furthermore, I've yet to meet a parent who, in the absence of clear evidence to the contrary, didn't think his or her child was average or above in the intelligence department. The sobering fact of the matter is that out of four randomly selected children, only two are likely to be "average." Of the other two, one will probably be above average, and one will probably be below average. Average means the middle, which means that for every child who is above average, there is one who is correspondingly below.

The second question—"Are this child's skills in reading, language arts, and math on a par with his/her ability level?"— is answered by comparing the obtained measure of ability with the child's performance on the academic skills assessment. If there's a match—in other words, if the child's academic skills line up with his/her ability level, and ability level is average to above—then the child's school performance problems are probably due to a lack of motivation. However, if motivation of the sort described in Chapter Three has been tried without success, then the problem may be related to stress, depression, or other emotional factors. If that possibility exists, the child's psychological condition should be assessed by a child psychologist or psychiatrist.

The third question—"Are the child's skills such that he/she is presently capable of doing grade level work in school?"—is answered by comparing the child's scores on the academic achievement tests with what's expected of the average child in the same grade.

At this point, you should have enough of an information base upon which to make some sound decisions.

Okay, you can read the next three chapters now.

Chapter Four

When to Remediate

Remediation consists of providing a child with academic instruction over and above what he or she is receiving in a regular classroom setting.

Remediation is called for if . . .

- the child's academic skills, in one or more areas, test significantly below *ability* level.
- the child's ability level is average or above, but certain academic skills are below grade level.
- significant inconsistencies exist between the child's achievement levels in reading, language arts, spelling, and math.

Keep in mind that it's entirely possible, and not at all unusual, for a child to test at or above grade level, but below ability. Therefore, the mere fact that a child's academic skills are commensurate with grade-level expectations does not rule out the advisability of remediation.

A significant discrepancy between achievement level and ability might result from a learning disability, depression or other emotional factors, a long-standing motivational disturbance, excessive television-watching, or a general indifference toward education on the part of the child's parents. It might also mean that the child got off to a bad start in school from which he never fully recovered. Regardless, if efforts are not made to realign achievement and ability, the problem is likely to deteriorate further. If the child's self-esteem was not at risk to begin with, it eventually will be.

In some cases, the child may qualify for extra help through an in-school special education or "resource" program. The guidelines for qualification vary from state to state, but in every instance a significant discrepancy between ability level and skill level is the central requirement.

Remediation can also be obtained by contracting with a private tutor, in which case the extra help is delivered on a one-on-one basis outside of school. Within recent years, a number of private tutoring programs have sprung up around the country. Also known as "learning centers," they provide remedial help in groups of three to five children.

The advantages of having a child receive remedial help from a school-based special education program are . . .

- the teachers are highly qualified and receive continuing education on a regular basis;
- there is a virtual guarantee of close communication between the special education teacher and the classroom teacher;
- in-school programs are "free" and convenient.

The problem, however, with in-school programs is that a child cannot receive help through them simply because he needs it. Ideally, of course, every child should be able to receive a "special" education tailored to his or her individual strengths and weaknesses, but as things stand, in order to qualify a child for in-school assistance, it must be shown that the child is "handicapped" in one way or another. In the absence of mental retardation, severe behavior problems, chronic health problems, or physical handicap, the underachieving child is most likely to qualify as "learning disabled" or "LD."

The manner in which public schools use the term "learning disabled" can be, however, highly misleading. The fact that a child qualifies for an LD program does not necessarily mean that the child has a neurological (central nervous system-based) or developmental (maturational) dysfunction of one kind or other that interferes with effective learning. It may simply mean that a significant gap exists between the child's ability level and his or her level of academic proficiency, and that the gap has not responded to traditional, classroom-based interventions. As I've already said, a discrepancy of this sort demands remediation, but does not necessarily justify attaching a diagnosis of learning disabled to the child.

Under the circumstances, even if a child legitimately qualifies for a special education program, I am generally not in favor of securing remediation through the schools. To begin with, I don't like the fact that children can't get into these programs without first being labeled as handicapped, especially when that may not be the case at all.

Second, it's hard to tell just how much progress a child is actually making in a special education program. Once a child is in a program of this sort, report card grades usually improve because the child is being evaluated against lowered academic expectations. The parents see the improved grades and think progress is being made, when in fact it may not be.

I've come across many children who, after several years of part-time work in resource programs, were still well behind in their skills. By the time this fact was brought to light, the majority of these kids had lost so much ground that they could never catch up without being retained. And even if retained, they had lost so much confidence in themselves, and so much interest in school, that *complete* academic rehabilitation had become a virtual impossibility.

"So why," one might ask, "didn't the schools just retain them to begin with?"

That's an interesting question, and one we'll look at in more depth in the next chapter. Suffice at this point to say that most school systems will either remediate or retain, but they won't do both. This one-or-the-other policy means that a child who needs to be retained, and whose problems could have been solved much more easily *had* he been retained, is moved along from one grade to the next because it's determined he's "learning disabled" and the powers-that-be believe retention would deliver the killing blow to his self-esteem. So, to protect his supposedly fragile psyche, they waste his valuable time. God and the educational bureaucracy move in mysterious ways.

The defenders of these programs claim that these are children who would become "lost" in the regular classroom. Ah, but recent studies have found that children tend to make more rapid progress if they are *not* grouped homogeneously; that is, according to ability. The latest findings suggest that even kids with very low skills tend to do better when they remain in heterogenous groupings and receive whatever individual help they need before or after school.

The last, but not the least, of my objections to these programs is the fact that during the time the child is receiving remedial help, he's missing whatever instruction is taking place in the regular classroom. It might be, for instance, that while a child is receiving an hour of remedial work in reading through a resource program, he's missing an hour of spelling and language arts instruction in the classroom, instruction for which he will nonetheless be held accountable. This "rob Peter to pay Paul" aspect effectively cancels whatever benefit the child *might* be getting while in the resource program.

I'm not alone in my opinions and feelings about in-school special education programs and the practice of requiring that children be labeled as handicapped in order to receive special assistance. In late 1989, the National Association of School Psychologists (NASP), a first-rate professional organization with first-order knowledge and influence in this area, released a statement which questioned the practice of requiring that "children be labeled as handicapped and removed from regular classrooms to receive special assistance." NASP called upon school systems to begin taking steps to integrate special services and support programs within the regular classroom.

For all these reasons, I generally recommend that remedial help, when needed, be obtained through private tutors or learning centers. Granted, these options are more expensive and certainly not as convenient, but as things now stand, they involve fewer complications and undesirable "side effects" than do in-school programs.

Which is generally better, a private tutor or a learning center? Depends on how you look at it. Private tutors are usually less expensive than learning centers, simply because they incur less overhead expense. They also work one-on-one with the child whereas in a learning center, one teacher will usually work simultaneously with several children. Instead of providing true remediation, however, many private tutors end up providing nothing more than homework assistance and support. While this may help the child keep up in school, it fails to get to the "bottom" of the child's problem, and is only slightly more helpful than having a parent sit and do homework with the child night after night.

A private tutor usually brings a bit more of a warm "personal touch" into his or her work with a child. That, if it doesn't overshadow the tasks at hand, can be extremely motivating. Nevertheless, when contracting with a private tutor, parents need to make their expectations explicit. Make it clear that you are contracting for remediation, not fun and games, and ask the tutor to give you a written plan of what she plans to accomplish with your child, how, and according to what timetable.

If you're going to opt for a private tutor, make sure you find a person who has a proven reputation and is certified to teach at your child's grade level and/or the subject or subjects under discussion. Ask your child's principal or guidance counselor if they have a list of "approved" tutors to whom they regularly refer.

Learning centers are the more expensive alternative. My experience has been that they are also, in the long run, the most cost-effective. A service-oriented business must produce results in order to stay in business, and that rule applies to a learning center as well as a dry cleaners. As a consequence, most learning centers are truly remedial in philosophy and practice. They don't just help the child keep up. They help him *catch up* in his skills so he can keep up on his own. Furthermore, a reputable learning center will have at its disposal an extensive library of instructional materials, something a private tutor is unlikely to have at her disposal, which means that the staff can adapt far more flexibly to a broad range of learning styles.

As with anything else, however, there are good learning centers and there are ones that are not so good. When shopping, look for a center that . . .

- comes highly recommended by other parents and professionals (pediatricians, psychologists, etc.);
- has been in business more than two years;
- employs teachers who are state-certified and have classroom experience;
- guarantees your child will be working with a teacher who is certified to teach at your child's grade level and in the subjects in which need exists;
- uses a variety of learning materials, thus enabling adaptation to a broad range of learning styles;
- uses computer-assisted instruction as a *supplement* to teacher-based instruction, rather than as a primary instructional technique;
- retests your child periodically to check his/her progress;
- guarantees they will contact and continue to communicate with your child's regular classroom teacher;
- promises to keep you regularly posted concerning your child's progress in their program.

Questions?

Q: Up until this year, my child was in a private school operated by a local fundamentalist church. We put Robbie there because they claimed that with small classes and an accelerated curriculum, their students were achieving at least one grade level above kids in public school. Robbie went there from kindergarten through third grade and always made nearly straight A's. At that point, we moved to a new community and put him in public school. His fourth-grade teacher called us in for a conference several weeks after school started and told us that Robbie's language arts and math skills were not what they should be and that he would need extra help. In fact, she said that if she had known this prior to the start of school, she'd have recommended that he repeat the third grade. How can this be?

A: It can be because it takes more than small classes and an accelerated curriculum to get an entire group of children of different ability levels to perform one grade level above public school expectations. It takes an act of God, which even a church-operated school cannot order at will.

I find that many small, church-operated schools make this same claim. (Note: I am not lumping all church-operated schools together. There are ones that are reputable and ones that are not so reputable and, generally speaking, the greater the hype, the less reputable the school.) They create the illusion of higher achievement levels by beginning academic instruction in kindergarten, focusing on memorization instead of comprehension and concept formation, and emphasizing rote drill over exploratory learning experiences. Indeed, they're generally successful at infusing children with lots of facts, but not at helping children learn how to synthesize those facts creatively. In reading, word recognition is stressed over passage comprehension. In writing, grammar and punctuation are stressed over creative expression. In 'rithmetic, facts are stressed over application of concepts.

Obviously, you can't undo what's already been done. Your son needs extra help, and fast! You should count your lucky stars the public school didn't discover the problem prior to the start of the new school year. Assuming he's capable, retention isn't the answer, and would probably have created more problems than it solved.

Contract with a reputable private tutor or learning center

to work with your son after school. In either case, the tutor or center needs to do a thorough evaluation of your son's academic skills before developing a remedial plan. Make sure, before entering into a contract, that the center/tutor has a clear picture of the problem, and is able to articulate a clear set of goals along with a concrete set of remedial strategies.

Q: You seem to be saying that there are risks involved in putting children in private school. Are there certain children who *need* private education? If so, how do you identify them? Also, what should parents look for if they're shopping for private schools?

A: Don't misunderstood me. There are no definite, across-the-board risks involved in putting children in private schools. There are, however, risks involved in putting children in *certain* private schools.

The better private schools provide an important, worthwhile alternative to public education. Their classrooms are generally smaller, the attention is usually a bit more personalized, the level of communication between teachers and parents is generally better than you find in a public setting, and they often are able to better meet the needs of those children whose talents might not be recognized and cultivated in public school.

The first thing parents should remember when shopping for private schooling is that reputable private schools don't make outrageous claims. They don't need to. They don't claim to be the answer for everybody, just an alternative for some. They don't act like they're in competition with public schools, because they're not. They don't claim to be better, just different. In general, the stronger the school's "come on," the more skeptical parents should be.

Before making a private-school decision, make sure . . .

97

- the school is accredited by a reputable educational association;
- all teachers are state-certified and attend continuing education programs on a regular basis;
- the curriculum matches, but does not necessarily exceed, that found in local public schools;
- a full-time guidance counselor is on staff;
- community professionals give the school high marks;
- the school is able to provide extra help—again, outside regular classroom hours—to children who need it.

Q: Our son was an excellent student until this year, when he started seventh grade at the local junior-high school. Almost immediately, his grades took a nose dive. The problem is, he doesn't seem the least bit concerned. We don't understand how a child who took such pride in making good grades could now be so nonchalant about bad ones. If he wasn't so popular, we'd think perhaps we were dealing with poor self-esteem. What's going on, and what should we do?

A: In all likelihood, what's going on is what I call "seventh-grade slump." The transition between elementary school and junior high or what's sometimes called "middle" school can be extremely problematic for some children. Junior-high teachers tend to be more subject-oriented than student-oriented, students change classes throughout the day, and teachers are less able, and (unfortunately) sometimes less willing, to give individual attention—all this means that children are rather suddenly expected to be considerably more responsible and self-starting than they were just one year before. Add to this the fact that junior-high students are typically paying more attention to social standing than academic standing, and you've got the makings of a potential mess.

If your son were less popular, I might suggest the self-esteem hypothesis myself. The paradoxical nature of junior high is such that socially unsuccessful kids quite often become depressed, which results in poor grades, while socially successful kids spend the majority of their time cultivating their social lives, which results in poor grades. What's a parent to do?

This is probably a simple case of misplaced priorities, in which case it's unlikely that your son needs anything more than for you to light a strong fire underneath him. Chapter Three contains suggestions that might prove helpful.

Q: Just exactly what is a learning disability?

A: I'll tell you what a learning disability *is*, then I'll tell you what it *isn't*.

The term *learning disability* refers to an insidious neurological or developmental problem which handicaps a child's ability to perform up to his or her potential in school.

Learning disabilities are *insidious* because they are not immediately apparent to the naked eye, as are many other handicaps, such as cerebral palsy. Some learning disabilities are due to *neurological* problems, or minor malfunctions within the circuitry of the central nervous system. Others are *developmental*, meaning they are the result of maturational problems, as opposed to disease or injury.

Effective learning requires the successful integration of perceptual (sensory), cognitive (intellectual), and motor processes. Information enters the body through the perceptual system (eyes, ears, etc.), is processed by the cognitive system (brain), and is responded to by the motor system (muscles). A dysfunction of one sort or another in this sequence will prevent the effective coordination of those systems and interfere with effective learning. That's what we call a learning disability.

There are as many kinds of learning disabilities as there are neurological and maturational areas which impact learning and, therefore, school performance. These include fine-motor coordination, various cognitive (problem-solving) processes, visual tracking, communication skills, and attention span—to mention but a few.

It's important to understand just exactly what the word *disability*, in this particular context, means. It does *not*, as many people seem to think, imply an *in-ability* of any sort. Rather it refers to a *disruption* of ability. So, when someone says that a child has an auditory processing disability, this doesn't mean the child *cannot* learn by listening, just that the child has relative difficulty learning through strictly auditory channels.

The word *disability* also creates the impression that these problems are insurmountable, permanent; that we cannot reasonably expect the same level of academic performance from learning-disabled (LD) children that we can from non-LD children; that LD children require esoteric teaching methods and materials, and so on. I haven't found this to be true. A learning-disabled child may have to put more time and effort into learning certain tasks, but he or she is capable of learning just as much and performing just as well as the next child of equivalent ability. Indeed, LD children often do need remedial assistance of one sort or another, but that is usually the extent to which anything special needs to be done for them.

The *last* thing an LD child needs is adults who, out of sympathy, help him avoid certain tasks just because those tasks are frustrating. The fact is that whatever the LD child's weakness or weaknesses, they can be strengthened, and therefore remediated, *only* by exposing the child to the very tasks that give him the greatest degree of difficulty. Unfortunately, most LD specialists teach predominantly to the child's strengths. This certainly *sounds* like the right thing to do, and indeed, should be part of the overall remedial plan. Recognize, however, that teaching to the child's strengths is *compensatory* in nature, and as I said in Chapter One, you can't compensate for a problem and correct it at the same time. Teaching strictly to the child's strengths may successfully conceal the consequences of the problem, but it also allows the child's weaknesses to get that much weaker.

Learning disabilities are not permanent. They are correctable. In order to retrain an LD child's central nervous system or help him overcome maturational deficiencies, the teacher/therapist should employ a supportive, patient teaching style along with materials and exercises aimed at strengthening the child's weaknesses, rather than simply building compensations around them.

More than anything else, the LD child's parents and teachers should always expect the child to persevere in the face of his or her personal adversity. In effect, a learning disability is a *challenge* and should be affirmed as such.

The danger in treating these kids as if they were victims of circumstances beyond their control is that treatment of that sort tends to be self-fulfilling. You treat a child as if he has an excuse not to work up to normal expectations and pretty soon, he incorporates that excuse into his self-concept. The end result: Instead of a "can do" kid, you've got a "can't do" kid.

Q: You seem to be saying that your ABC's of effective homework management should be used with even learning-disabled kids. Am I getting this right?

A: You're getting it right. But LD kids need more than just my Homework ABC's. They need remediation as well, and if the problem has gone undetected for a relatively long period of time, retention might also be called for. Furthermore, some LD children also have attention deficit disorder (ADD), in which case the possibility of putting the child on medication might also need to be considered (see Chapter Six).

Q: Our nine-year-old son was recently tested at school and found to be learning-disabled. The school wants Sammy to work with the special education teacher an hour a day, outside the classroom. How do you feel about this?

A: I recommend that you have an independent psychologist—one with expertise in the area of learning problems—look over the evaluation done by the school and give you a second opinion. This recommendation has nothing whatsoever to do with the quality of evaluations done by school psychologists, because they are generally excellent, but with the criteria public schools use to identify learning-disabled children.

In some public school systems, the criteria used to determine whether a child is or is not LD produce occasional "false positives"—children who aren't truly LD, but whose test results qualify them as such. Bureaucratic definitions also fail to catch many truly LD children during their first two years in school, when remedial efforts will be most successful.

Again, these problems have to do with policies, not people. As a group, school psychologists are well-trained, competent professionals, every bit as capable as psychologists in private practice. The difficult dilemma they face is that they must juggle the limitations of the system, their employer, alongside the needs of the children in the system. The majority of school psychologists are doing the best job they can under the circumstances. The circumstances, however, don't always allow school psychologists to do the job they're capable of doing.

The National Association of School Psychologists recognizes these problems and has recently taken assertive steps to do something about them. NASP is urging schools to recognize that children learn in different ways and that a difference in learning style is not necessarily a disability. They're also asking that schools begin integrating special services into the regular classroom setting. The changes that they're advocating will take time, as all institutional change does, but will be worth the wait.

If you see an independent psychologist, and he/she feels

Sammy would benefit from extra help, I'd recommend that you look into getting him the remedial help he needs through a private tutor or learning center rather than through an in-school "pull-out" program. If you choose, for whatever reasons, to let the school remediate, then make sure Sammy isn't going to be pulled out of class during prime instructional time.

Q: Our six-year-old started first grade this fall. We've noticed that on quite a few papers he's written certain letters backward. He did this a lot last year, but when we expressed concern about it, his teacher told us it was nothing to worry about. At the first PTA night this year, we met his new teacher. She also mentioned the reversals, but told us she thinks Brian is "seeing things backward," a symptom of dyslexia. She recommended that we have him tested. At this point, we are thoroughly confused. Do we have something to worry about or not?

A: Yes, I'd say you do have something to worry about, but it's not the fact that Brian reverses his letters. You should worry about his first-grade teacher, who has jumped to a very wrong conclusion. The problem is that her "diagnosis," wrong as it is, could be damaging to Brian. There is, for instance, the very real danger that she will communicate to him her feeling that something is wrong. If this happens, he may lose confidence in himself and develop performance anxiety, which will surely interfere with his learning potential. Research has clearly demonstrated that a teacher's perceptions and expectations can significantly influence a child's behavior, school performance, and even IQ!

The notion that children who make certain letter reversals are seeing things backwards became widespread in the 1970s. Despite the fact that it borders on the absurd, it persists. If these children truly saw things backward, they would forever be walking into walls, in which case a symptom of dyslexia would be a flat, chronically bruised face.

Even if they *did* see letters backward, they would still write them correctly. Think about it. Say, for instance, that for a certain child, "d's" look like "b's." When this child went to write a "d," therefore, he would write it so that it would look, to him, like a "b," which is to say he would write a "d." In other words, if there existed children who saw letters backwards, no one would ever know, and the "problem" would cause these children no difficulties whatsoever.

The truth is, lots of six-year-olds reverse certain letters. In fact, letter reversals are fairly common in children through age eight. As one might expect, they occur most often with the letters b, d, e, g, j, p, q, s, y, and z. In most of these cases, the visual difference between one letter and the other is subtle and difficult to remember. So a child innocently substitutes "d" for "b" and "p" for "q."

An actual reversal, which might occur with "e" or "s," usually happens simply because the child forgot for the moment the direction the letter faces. In addition, some children may have an initial tendency to turn almost all the letters of the alphabet in the same direction.

Regardless of the reason these reversals and substitutions occur, they merit no worry. A patient teaching approach will usually correct the problem within a relatively short period of time. The child makes a reversal or substitution, the teacher gently points it out, the child corrects it, and the proper habit slowly but surely develops.

On the other hand, if a big deal is made about the reversals, if the child senses that people are concerned, he could easily become confused, insecure, and anxious about his school performance. The end result could very well be a child with learning problems. That's why it's so important that you resolve this issue with the teacher. If you find that you can't, then do what you must to see that Brian is transferred to another first-grade classroom where there is a teacher who doesn't make mountains out of molehills.

When to Remediate

Q: Several years ago, we suspected that my son had a learning disability. The literature we read and the experts we talked to all said that letter reversal is a sure sign of dyslexia, as well as a symptom of other learning disabilities. You say it isn't. Who should we believe?

A: To say that letter reversal is a symptom of dyslexia is like saying that a cough is a symptom of pneumonia. A child can have a cough without pneumonia, and a child can reverse letters without being learning-disabled. In fact, only a small number of children who reverse letters are eventually found to have serious learning problems. Furthermore, just as it's possible to have pneumonia *without* a cough, the absence of letter reversals is no guarantee a child *isn't* LD.

Q: What, then, are the tell-tale symptoms of learning disabilities?

A: There are no clear tell-tale symptoms. There are only *indications*. If enough indications are present, it is reasonable to arrive at the conclusion that, yes, the child in question has a learning disability.

A partial list of these indications follows, but please read them with caution! The fact that a child exhibits some of these characteristics doesn't necessarily mean he or she is learning-disabled. However, if many or most of the items are descriptive of your child, you should have him evaluated by a psychologist who has experience and expertise in the field of learning problems. The earlier the detection, the better the chances the problem can be corrected. All of these symptoms assume a child of at least average intelligence.

• Capable of at least average achievement, but performing significantly below ability level in most, if not all, academic subjects.

- Difficulty understanding and carrying out directions, whether written or oral.
- General sequencing problems (e.g., difficulty keeping the days of the week or months of the year in order).
- Problem-solving attempts are generally inflexible or disorganized, reflecting inadequate trial-and-error skills.
- Problems with short-term memory (forgetful, "absent-minded").
- Asks a lot of unnecessary or self-evident questions.
- Frequently misunderstands what people say.
- Problems with fine-motor coordination (e.g. poor handwriting, immature drawings, "all thumbs").
- Problems with gross-motor coordination (clumsy, "trips over his own feet")
- Difficulty organizing ideas and expressing them orally and/or in writing.
- Difficulty with phonics (decoding, sequencing, and blending phonetic sounds).
- Difficulty with reading comprehension.
- Easily frustrated by schoolwork, has developed an "I can't" attitude.
- And finally, what some LD experts have termed "the most obvious symptom of all"—poor spelling skills.

I should also mention that a significant number of LD children are also found, upon examination, to have what are called "soft" signs of neurological (central nervous system) dysfunction, meaning that there are "fuzzy" indications of slight neurological impairment, but no hard-and-fast evidence.

Q: Our eight-year-old son has dyslexia. As a result, he's already more than a year behind in reading skills. We recently watched a talk show featuring a learning-disabilities specialist who said most, if not all, learning disabilities were inherited. Is this true?

A: There are many different kinds of learning disabilities, and it is *not* true that most are transmitted genetically. Some may, in fact, be hereditary, while others may be induced *in utero* by, say, the mother's use or overuse of drugs, tobacco, alcohol, even coffee. Some may result from prematurity, others from inadequate nutrition during infancy and early childhood.

I happen to believe that most—but by no means all—learning disabilities can be explained in developmental terms. In other words, children develop specific learning disabilities as a result of not having had adequate opportunity to exercise certain important skills during their formative years (birth through age 6). As a result, these skills fail to adequately strengthen. In school, these maturational deficiencies translate into problems learning to read, write, understand directions, and so on.

Since the early 1950s, learning disabilities have become epidemic among school-age children in America. Many believe the sharp increase is due to better identification procedures. I don't. I think we've had to put more effort into research and identification *because* of the increase. Better identification procedures don't *cause* epidemics; they come about as a result of them.

It's interesting to note that learning disabilities are not nearly as much a problem in European school-age populations as they are in the United States. Since we share much of the same gene pool, this would seem to minimize a genetic explanation and suggest that the reason for this country's epidemic may be largely cultural or environmental.

The question then becomes: "What are the most typical differences in upbringing between European and American children?"

There are many, to be sure, but one of the most striking has to do with television. By and large, European children watch less than five hours of television a week, and American children watch between twenty-five and thirty. Can large amounts of television cause learning disabilities? Developmental theory strongly suggests it can.

A vast array of skills and talents is contained within the

human genetic code. In order to activate this program, the preschool child must be exposed to environments and experiences that promote the exercise of those talents. In other words, the more creatively active the child is during his or her preschool—or formative—years, the more talented he or she will eventually be.

Watching television is a *passivity*, not an activity. It does not properly engage any human potential—motor, intellectual, creative, social, sensory, verbal, or emotional. Therefore, by its very nature, and regardless of the program, television is a *deprivational* experience for the formative-years child.

Reading is not *one* skill, but a *collection* of skills. In order to learn to read well, a child must come to the task with the complete set. If certain pieces are missing or damaged, learning to read will be that much more frustrating for the child.

The average American child has watched six thousand hours of television before he enters first grade. Think of it! Can we truly expect that the necessary set of skills can endure that amount of developmental deprivation and survive intact?

And let us not forget that so-called learning disabled-children are only the tip of the "Why-Can't-Johnny-Read?" iceberg. Since the early fifties, scholastic achievement measures have slipped steadily downhill and illiteracy has risen to affect nearly one out of five seventeen-year-olds.

Could our love affair with television be lurking behind our national reading crisis? We may never know for sure. The question is, is it worth the risk?

Chapter Five

When to Retain

It used to be called "failing" or "flunking." More recently, it's come to be known as "retention" or "non-promotion." Regardless, it's the practice of requiring a child to repeat a particular grade in school. These days, however, any discussion of the subject must also include the issue of delaying an age-appropriate child's entrance into kindergarten.

The use of retention was first associated with the introduction of graded schools in the nineteenth century and developed in response to the problem of students who seemed ill-prepared for moving successfully on to the next grade level. Concern about the possible negative effects of holding a child back was first expressed in the 1930s; nevertheless, retention continued to be fairly common and widespread.

In the late 1960s and well into the 1970s, retention became less popular as schools sought alternative ways of managing children with academic problems. As the seventies drew to a close, however, there was once again an upswing in the number of children being retained. Since then, retentions have continued to rise.

Interestingly enough, more children are now being retained in kindergarten than in any other grade. From 1979 to 1985, in those states that keep such records, the number of children repeating kindergarten (after adjusting for fluctuations in the overall kindergarten population) increased nearly sixty percent. Most kindergarten-retained children are either chronologically young when they enter school—so-called "late-birthday" children—or, regardless of birthdate, exhibit slight maturational shortcomings at the end of their first kindergarten year. Among advocates, the general feeling is that an extra year in kindergarten gives these children time to catch up in developmental skills before starting first grade, thus reducing the risk of later school failure.

Once upon a time, not so long ago, most educators agreed that retaining a child in one of the early elementary grades (K-3)—and kindergarten in particular—wasn't likely to damage the child's self-esteem. Early retention also gave the immature child an additional year to catch up maturationally. Furthermore, because the material was already familiar, retention gave the child an invaluable opportunity to experience academic success on the second "go-round." This positive experience would, it was argued, form the foundation for continued school achievement.

Early retention of this sort has come under heavy fire of late from many educators, and the ensuing debate has inspired some strong language. Commenting on the finding, in one study, that kindergarten-retained children had more academic, social, and emotional problems later than did a comparable group of children who had been promoted to first grade, a well-known and highly respected educator (who shall remain unnamed) pronounced, "Keeping kids back in kindergarten is immoral."

If that's the case, then I know plenty of immoral kindergarten teachers. Not long ago, a Long Beach, California, teacher wrote me a relatively long confessional in which she admitted to having retained seven—that's right, *seven*—"late-birthday" children in one year. She wrote:

> "I asked them if they would like to stay with me another year, and they all said they would. They were of at least average intelligence. Their only 'handicap' was their late birthdays. Their parents were in favor of the decision to retain. The next year, the children all had a wonderful kindergarten experience and were ready and eager for first

grade. As you might imagine, I am in total favor of retention in certain cases, and I know seven happy children who can back up my opinion!"

To this teacher's testimonial, I can add my own. Over the last fifteen years, I've had a hand in retaining more than a few kindergarten children. Without exception, those children benefited from a second year in kindergarten. I'm quite sure that, had they been moved prematurely to first grade, many of those same kids would have fallen further and further behind, would eventually have been placed in special education programs, and might not ever have realized their potential.

I recently evaluated a kindergarten child who was having problems associated with some slight developmental delays. It was late in the year, the teacher had recommended retention, and the parents wanted my opinion. The results of my evaluation convinced me that the little boy would not be ready for first grade in the fall. I concurred, therefore, with the teacher's recommendation. Nonetheless, the parents went ahead and advanced him to the first grade. Six weeks into the year, they called to tell me that the first-grade teacher had already talked with them about having their son tested to determine his eligibility for special services.

"What do we do now?" they asked.

Unfortunately, because they hadn't taken my original advice, they were now between a rock and a hard place. Since their son had already started first grade and looked forward to going to school, we were past the point of putting him back in kindergarten. I didn't want to see him labeled and put in a special education program, especially in light of the fact that his problems would probably have resolved had he been retained. After much discussion among all concerned, the less-than-satisfactory decision was made to let him stay in first grade, but retain him at the end of the year. This fiasco points up the kinds of problems that can occur when a child should be retained, but isn't.

One of the most rational and reasonable voices in this

debate belongs to Dr. James K. Uphoff of Wright State University's College of Education and Human Services and author of the book, *Summer Children: Ready or Not for School* (1986).

Uphoff charges, and correctly so, that the K-3 curriculum in most American public schools is developmentally inappropriate for large numbers of children. Noting that in many kindergartens, children are receiving instruction that was once reserved for first grade, Uphoff laments, "While the rush was on, we forgot to tell Mother Nature that she had to speed up the growth and development of children so they could cope with these new and inappropriate expectations.

"Being bright and being ready to begin formal academic instruction are two very separate issues," he says. "When children enter school before they are developmentally ready to cope with the academic expectations, their chances for failure increase dramatically."

Uphoff recognizes that change, although now widely acknowledged as necessary, will take place slowly within the educational bureaucracy. In the meantime, he calls for the creation of educational options that will guarantee success for young children whose readiness level is not yet suited to the demands of what he terms the "push-down" curriculum. He calls these alternatives—delayed kindergarten enrollment, developmental "pre-K" programs for four-year-olds and five-year-olds with late birthdays, and transitional programs between kindergarten and first grade—"gift of time" options.

Uphoff feels that these alternatives, all of which are specifically intended to provide "immature" children with early success experiences, work better than retention. But, he says, if retention is the only option, the earlier the better. A number of studies support his position. One such study, conducted in California, compared children retained in kindergarten with those whose parents declined the recommendation and sent them directly on to first grade. A follow-up evaluation found significantly higher achievement levels persisting through grade three for the retained group. Another study of over six-hundred children in Minnesota found that both self-concept and achievement were significantly lower among children for whom a growth year was recommended and *not* taken.

When he compared children who entered school when they were chronogically young—he calls them "summer children" because their birthdays occur in June, July, August, or September—with children who were older at school entrance, Uphoff found:

• Chronologically older children in a grade tend to receive more above-average grades than do younger children in the same grade.
• Older children are much more likely to score in the above-average range on standardized achievement tests.
• The younger children in a grade are more likely to eventually be labeled "learning disabled" than older students in the same grade.
• The early academic problems frequently experienced by "summer children" often follow them throughout their school careers, and sometimes even into adulthood.

For these reasons, Uphoff generally recommends that late-birthday or summer children be given one of the three gift-of-time options already mentioned. If, on the other hand, a child's developmental unreadiness is not detected in time, and early retention becomes necessary, Uphoff recommends that parents present that decision to the child in terms that are not only positive, but also self-incriminating. For example, parents might say to a child, "We made a mistake. We started you in school too early, before you were ready. Repeating (the grade in question) will give you a chance to catch up with yourself, so that learning can be more fun and easier for you."

The only disagreement I have with Uphoff's position, and it's a slight one, concerns delayed kindergarten enrollment. If a child is eligible for kindergarten, even if he has a late birthday or some obvious, but relatively slight, immaturity, and the kindergarten is developmental rather than academic, I say enroll him. A tremendous amount of maturation can, and does, take place that year. Even without special attention, kindergarten children who are somewhat "behind" can, and do, catch up. For that reason, I prefer giving the child the benefit of the doubt. If at the end of kindergarten it's determined that he's not ready for first grade, either retain or, if there's one available, put him in a transitional "K-1" program. This all hinges, however, on the kindergarten program in question being developmental in nature. If the primary emphasis is on academics, then I'm in favor of delayed enrollment along with a year in a developmental "pre-K" program of one sort or another.

I've seen, and been party to, many instances when retention—even when it occurred relatively late—proved extremely helpful. My experience tells me that it's more appropriate for certain academically troubled students than for others. Unfortunately, retention is often employed as an expedient when other intervention options might well have solved the child's academic problems. The proper question is, "For what children and under what conditions is retention most likely to be successful?" In this regard, I find that retention stands the greatest chance of working when . . .

- it's done during the early elementary years (K-3);
- the child is or has fallen significantly behind in developmental and/or academic skills and individual tutoring (prescriptive education) is no longer a realistic option;
- factors other than ability are the cause of the child's academic difficulties.
- other therapeutic and remedial interventions are used in conjunction with retention to address those difficulties. This recognizes that retention never *solves* a child's problems—it only provides a context within which those problems *can* be solved.

Under these circumstances, I find that retention can result in considerable benefit to a child, assuming it is handled supportively and positively by both the child's parents and the teacher. Unfortunately, whether intended or not, many re-tained children hear the message, "You failed." The inevitable result is damage to self-esteem and the desire to achieve. When a child is made to feel that retention is punishment for doing poorly in school, it isn't going to work.

Almost all rules have their exceptions, and the following story illustrates one such example: A number of years ago, the parents of a sixth-grade boy asked my advice concerning problems their son was having in school. He was small for his age and obviously self-conscious and defensive concerning his size. He had difficulties getting along with other children, his classroom behavior was frequently disruptive, and he'd fallen nearly two years behind in his academic development.

My evaluation indicated that he had the ability to do above-average work in school. In all likelihood, a combination of factors had "snowballed" to throw him off track. He was probably an appropriate candidate for retention in kindergarten or first grade, but then again, had his difficulties been identified and addressed early enough, that might not have been necessary. All of that, however, was water over the dam. The question now was how to best help him at this stage of the game.

After careful consideration of all the options, I recommended that he be retained in the sixth grade and given remedial help outside of school during that following year. My decision turned on the fact that seventh grade meant a move to junior high school, where he'd be changing classes throughout the day. Furthermore, junior high school teachers tend to be more subject- than student-oriented. Under the circumstances, I feared that this young fellow's problems would only become that much more difficult to "capture" and correct if he took them with him into seventh grade. Not only was he not mature enough to accept the responsibility expected at that level, he didn't have the skills to do the work. He would either have required remedial classes or more extra help than was realistically possible to provide.

Knowing that we were running a risk, and hoping to minimize it, I "coached" the parents concerning not only when and how to break the news to their son, but also how to respond supportively to his anger and anxieties. As we expected, he reacted explosively. He ranted and raved and even threatened to run away. The parents were patient, but firm. They accepted his feelings, were as reassuring as possible, and let his reaction run its course.

The following year, even though he came to school with a chip on his shoulder, the boy quickly discovered that his size was no longer a disadvantage in a younger group. He made friends quickly and became a leader both inside and outside the classroom. Furthermore, the fact that the work was familiar, combined with the extra help he was getting outside of school, made it relatively easy for him to make good grades. He began taking pride in his work and his improved behavior reflected vastly improved self-esteem.

I ran into the boy's parents several months ago. They told me that he had just completed his junior year in high school and was not only popular among his classmates but an "A" student as well. His mother said, "Being retained in the sixth grade was the best thing that ever happened to him."

The key ingredients in this youngster's successful retention were timing, parental support, and academic remediation. One thing is certain: To simply retain a child and do nothing to address the problems that contributed to the child's academic difficulties is irresponsible and will, in the long run, create more problems than it solves.

There is a widespread belief, even among professionals, that the retained child will forever look upon himself as a failure and sink slowly, but inexorably, to the level of that internal expectation. Frogfeathers! If you want to help a child who's falling behind in school develop a disabling attitude toward himself, you need only to continue promoting him from grade to grade. To create the illusion that he's being helped, have him tested and placed in a program where he receives special attention outside the regular classroom for a short time each day. Instead of protecting a child from feelings of failure, these manipulations virtually guarantee them.

My finding, based on nearly twenty years of accumulated anecdotal experience, is that a child who should have been retained in one of the early grades but wasn't, is likely to fall further and further behind his age-mates as the years march on. Eventually, overwhelmed by frustration and feelings of defeat, the child gives up altogether. He becomes apathetic toward school and often develops behavior problems. He finally succeeds in alienating himself from not only the system, but also from most of his peers, and contents himself with the easy company of other peripheral students. In all likelihood, this youngster will become an in-school dropout before age sixteen, and an actual dropout shortly thereafter.

The news, "You're going to be retained," is, indeed, initially traumatic for most children, but with adequate adult support the trauma is usually short-lived. Besides, as Dr. Louise Bates Aimes, Associate Director of the Gesell Institute of Human Development at Yale University, has said, "Even if it is traumatic to keep them back, it's better to traumatize them once and get it over with than to have them face problems every day for the next twelve years."

When I recommend retention, it is always in conjunction with other remedial approaches, including individualized prescriptive education (otherwise known as tutoring, covered in Chapter Four), motivational strategies (see Chapter Three), medication (see Chapter Six), and teaching parents the do's and don'ts of effective homework management. Note the conspicuous absence of counseling for the retained child. While many clinicians feel that counseling is necessary to soften the impact of retention, I have *never* found it to be necessary and believe that it can, in fact, be counterproductive. You treat a child as if he *ought* to be psychologically damaged from having been retained, and you run the risk of setting a self-fulfilling prophecy in motion. You can create a problem where there would have been none at all, or prolong a problem that would have otherwise run its course in a relatively short time.

Many psychologists, social workers, and guidance counselors are so wedded to the belief that the right sort of counsel ing can solve any problem that they fail to realize that the retained child may "hear" in the counseling process, the message, "You have a right to feel bad about what's happening to you." This perception, which the child would certainly not be able to articulate, would, nevertheless, have the effect of increasing the child's resistance to the retention and, therefore, negatively predisposing its outcome. My experience is that it's far more advantageous to teach the child's parents how to inform him or her of the decision to retain, acquaint them with the range of reactions possible (denial, sorrow, anger, blaming) which, interestingly enough, closely resemble the grieving process, and "coach" them concerning effective ways of responding to those behaviors.

Questions?

Q: Our son is one of the late-birthday kids you talk about. He's scheduled to start kindergarten this fall, but the program in our schools has a fairly heavy academic emphasis, especially during the second half of the year. If I take your advice and keep him out of school a year, is it going to make much difference whether I keep him at home or put him in a developmental preschool program?

A: I think it could make a big difference. There are several advantages to putting him in a developmental preschool program. First, because he'd be in a group of children his age, he'd make more gains in social and play skills than he would if he was simply at home. Second, because most of the activities would be structured and teacher-directed, a developmental preschool would prepare him better for the expectations his kindergarten teacher will have. Third, a developmental program incorporates activities that stimulate and strengthen specific developmental skills. The likelihood is, therefore, that he'll make more progress in such a program than he would at home.

There are, however, a number of helpful things you can be

doing with him at home. You can read to him at least thirty minutes a day. You can provide paints, crayons, and colored pencils for him to draw and color with. You can take him on nature walks as well as educational walks through various parts of the town you live in. You can prepare him for the responsibility of school by giving him a routine of chores to do around the home. And that's just for starters. His preschool teacher will be able to give you even more suggestions.

Q: Most of the psychologists and pediatricians in our community are advising parents of children who turn five after June 1 to delay by one year their enrollment in kindergarten. They maintain this all but guarantees a successful kindergarten experience for children who, by virtue of late birthdays, are somewhat immature. As the parents of a child who will be five in August, we would like to know your thoughts on this matter.

A: In the last ten years or so, the recommendation to delay kindergarten entrance for so-called "late-birthday" children has become fairly standard within the professional community. The original feeling was that such a delay was more important for late-birthday boys (at this age, boys tend to lag slightly behind girls in fine-motor skills, eye-hand coordination, and language development). Over time, however, the recommendation has expanded to include both boys and girls with late birthdays, also known as "summer children."

The growth in popularity of this particular recommendation has a lot to do with the fact that over the last ten to twenty years, kindergartens have tended to become increasingly academic. The "push-down" curriculum, as it is called, places increasing numbers of children at risk for early failure experiences. Waiting to introduce academic skills until children are six reduces that risk considerably.

This is why, when the kindergarten program in question

stresses academic skills over developmental readiness, I am generally in favor of delayed enrollment. If, on the other hand, the program is developmental in emphasis, then I see little point in delaying kindergarten entrance for the late-birthday child unless significant developmental delays are part of the picture.

Enrolling the slightly immature child in kindergarten when the law allows is, in my mind, a "nothing ventured, nothing gained" proposition. A child who begins the year slightly behind developmentally stands a fairly good chance of catching up by the end of the year. If that hoped for progress doesn't occur, then a second year in kindergarten may be appropriate (for even some early birthday kids).

Many parents who choose delayed enrollment are motivated by a desire to enhance their children's chances of "going to the head of the class." That stands a good chance of backfiring, particularly for a child who was ready to start school at age five, and who, that following year, is bored stiff in a kindergarten setting.

Furthermore, if delayed enrollment for "summer children" becomes the norm, then all we end up doing is creating a new group of late-birthday kids—those, in other words, with birthdays after March 1—who, relative to the rest of their kindergarten classmates, are "immature." If we carry this to its absurd extreme, then in another ten years or so children might not be entering kindergarten until age seven.

The most practical solution, or so it seems to me, is to first, stop pushing parts of the traditional first grade curriculum down into kindergarten; second, enroll all but significantly developmentally delayed children in kindergarten when the law says they can be enrolled; third, exercise the option of having certain children repeat kindergarten when that seems appropriate.

I should note that many schools are now offering transitional K-1 programs for children who need an additional readiness year before first grade. A tip of the hat to those innovative systems!

When to Retain

Q: Our son started kindergarten in September and turned five in October, only a few days prior to the deadline. Here it is November, and his teacher is already talking about having him repeat. It seems he isn't quite as mature as the rest of the kids, which is understandable, and that he isn't progressing as fast in his skills. How can we handle this without doing damage to his self-esteem?

A: It's a bit early to be making final decisions about who's going on to first grade and who isn't, but the teacher is right to let you know what she's thinking. Let's say you and the teacher eventually decide to have your son repeat. Will that mean you made a mistake by putting him in kindergarten this year? Hardly.

Your son will spend the year productively, advancing in his social skills, and being introduced to entry-level academic structure. The alternatives would have been to either keep him at home or put him in a preschool program for four- and young five-year-olds. Given that the kindergarten curriculum is developmental rather than academic, there isn't anything a developmental preschool could have done that kindergarten isn't doing. This way, there's at least a *chance* he'll be ready to go on to first grade on schedule.

If he's not, you needn't worry about damage to his self-esteem. The best and least disruptive time to have a child repeat is either in kindergarten or first grade. A child for whom early retention is appropriate will, in the long run, do far better socially, emotionally, and academically than he would have done otherwise.

Your son will handle the idea of spending another year in kindergarten as well as you handle it. If you act like there's something wrong, he'll think there's something wrong. If, on the other hand, you act like nothing's wrong, like spending a second year in the great and wonderful kindergarten place is no more significant than crossing the street, he'll shrug his shoulders and get on with it.

If the decision to retain is made, there's no need to give it a big, dramatic buildup. When the year is about over, his teacher should sit down with him and explain that since he's younger than the rest of the kids, she wants him to stay with her another year. And next year, since he'll be one of the oldest and will already know a lot about kindergarten, he can be a big help to her and the other kids. Won't that be just spiffy?

And he'll come home and tell you the good news and you'll be happy for him and that will be that. On the outside chance that he is upset, just reassure him that it's for the best and that things are going to be fine. If he sees that you're confident in the decision, he'll believe you. Trust is powerful good medicine.

Q: We recently applied for our son, age five, to attend kindergarten at a private elementary school in our community. After giving him a readiness test, they informed us that not only are his academic skills not up to their standards—he doesn't yet know his letters and numbers, for instance—but his fine-motor coordination is, as they put it, "slightly delayed." They even suggested he might have a learning disability. Even though they acknowledged he was bright, they said their program was not set up for the kinds of problems he might possibly experience in school. We left the interview feeling devastated. Does this sound serious to you? If so, where do we go from here?

A: What you've said doesn't sound serious to me at all, but please keep in mind that I'm in no position to determine whether or not your son has a developmental problem.

I am generally opposed to readiness testing with this age child, primarily because a child's developmental skills are still "in formation" at this age. This, in and of itself, raises doubts about the reliability of these tests and, therefore, any conclusions drawn from them.

There are a number of factors that can contaminate a

child's performance on a readiness test, including lack of familiarity with testing procedures, not understanding why the test is being given, and inadequate rapport with the examiner. Under the circumstances, there's a good chance that readiness testing will do nothing more than set off unwarranted false alarms. For that reason, they should be used conservatively, only by qualified professionals, and interpreted cautiously, with respect for their inherent limitations and drawbacks. If a readiness evaluation raises serious concerns about a child's developmental integrity, a more comprehensive evaluation should be done before making "career" decisions.

There is absolutely no substance to the popular notion that children should come to kindergarten already equipped with certain basic academic skills, including letter and number recognition and the ability to write their names. Recent research tends to indicate that not only is it inappropriate to apply these sorts of expectations at the preschool level but also potentially damaging. A premature attempt to push these skills can create problems that would not have developed otherwise. There are, in fact, a number of experts who believe that we are creating a fair number of learning disabilities by pushing literacy at children too early and too hard.

In this regard, it's interesting to note that in European and Russian school systems, where formal academic instruction doesn't generally begin until children are at least six, if not seven years old, the incidence of learning disabilities is virtually negligible, as is the incidence of illiteracy among seventeen-year-olds (the USA rate is one-in-five).

The fact that a five-year-old child falls below the norm with respect to the emergence of one or two developmental skills is not, in and of itself, anything to get excited about. If you looked hard enough, you could probably find "delays" of this sort with the majority of children this age. As I've already said, time and proper developmental programming are the great equalizers in situations of this sort. One year of developmentally appropriate kindergarten has helped many an "immature" child resolve these sorts of problems.

Where do you go from here? I'd go to the public schools in your community and ask about their kindergarten philosophy. If the emphasis is developmental, go ahead and put your son in their program. If it's academic, then it would probably be better to find a developmental "pre-K" program for him. At the end of that year, make a kindergarten decision.

Q: I'm a first-grade teacher who takes exception to your opinion that kindergartens should be developmental, rather than academic. The real push for children of kindergarten age to learn to read comes from the fact that first graders are expected to finish a certain standard of accomplishment—a set of primer books. If children do nothing but play for one year in a kindergarten setting, it's a real chore to accomplish the goals set for them in first grade.

A: First, the guided play activities typical of developmental kindergartens are not a waste of time, as your objection implies. They are creative, playful means of activating, exercising, and therefore strengthening all of the perceptual, motor, and cognitive skills children will need to become good readers. Developmental psychologists have long recognized that play is the most productive of all early childhood experiences.

Your remarks also contain the inference that the child should be made to conform to the timetable, rather than the timetable to the child. So, if the system decides children should have acquired a certain level of proficiency in reading by the end of first grade, and this level can't be achieved unless instruction begins in kindergarten, then instruction begins in kindergarten.

Teaching first-grade children to read will only be a "chore" if the system establishes unreasonable, unnecessary, and unrealistic goals. This, however, is exactly what school systems tend to do when they become more interested in improving their rank in the national achievement scores contest than they are in the needs of the children they are supposedly serving.

Your attitude, unfortunately commonplace among today's educators, is a perfect example of the reasoning behind the notion that the younger a child reads, the better. In general, Americans have a habit of judging the merit of things on the basis of product, or outcome, and ignoring the process by which that outcome is attained. This is particularly the case when it comes to evaluating things that directly affect our children, things like television and organized sports and early academics. In the latter case, it is a fact that kindergarten-age children can be taught to read. But the fact that it *can* be done does not necessarily mean that it *should* be done.

Jean Piaget, the eminent Swiss developmental psychologist, once spent a summer at Harvard studying with Jerome Bruner, the eminent American developmental psychologist. As Piaget was about to board ship for his return to Europe, a reporter asked his opinion of Bruner's contention that given proper instruction, any child could be taught any skill at virtually any age.

Piaget replied, "Only an American would think so."

Q: So what should parents be doing during the preschool years to help their children eventually become successful readers?

A: To begin with, parents need to realize that reading is not just one skill, but the interplay of many, including . . .

Inquiry: Reading is, first and foremost, an act of inquiry, exploration, and discovery. An inquisitive toddler rummages through drawers and cabinets in search of knowledge. In the same way, and for the same reasons, an inquisitive ten-year-old rummages through the pages of a book. Contrary to current mythology, learning to read is *easy*, assuming the child comes to the task equipped with the developmental tools needed to perform it.

Imagination: Reading ignites the imagination. A seven-year-old reader transforms words into images in much the same way a three-year-old transforms an old shoe box into a sailing ship. Imagination is essential to reading comprehension. It breathes life into the static word, making it dynamic. Without imagination, words are hollow. The child who has misplaced his imagination (or had it *displaced* by such things as watching too much television) will see reading as a chore, rather than a joy.

Coordination: Reading involves the coordination of perceptual, mental, and physical processes—eyes, brain, and hands. The eyes scan lines of print and transmit raw data to the brain. The brain processes that data—decoding, retrieving information stored in its vast data banks, making associations, and forming mental images, thus arriving at the "Ah-ha!" of understanding. Hands, meanwhile, hold the book, turn the pages, and adjust the depth of field so the eyes can focus.

Self-esteem: Reading, like any other meaningful activity, offers a child challenge. "He has good self-esteem" is really a roundabout way of saying, "He likes to be challenged." Reading, like every other challenge, offers a child the opportunity to grow in self-reliance and responsibility. Children with good self-esteem are in tune with the gentle art of growing.

A successful reader, therefore, is an inquisitive, imaginative, well-coordinated child with good self-esteem. There are three fundamental things parents *should* do to build these solid foundations:

First, parents should provide safe, stimulating environments that encourage inquiry and exploration. If, from his earliest months, a child's inquiries into the world are rewarding (as opposed to frustrating), and if parents feed (as opposed to deprive) his appetite for discovery, he will want, when the appropriate time comes, to rummage as eagerly through books as he did through drawers and cabinets when he was younger.

Second, parents should spend lots of time reading to children. And read with gusto! Breathe life into the story! Make the child's eyes grow wide with wonder at the power of the printed word! There are few things more completely enriching to a child—emotionally, socially, and intellectually—than being read to. Nestled securely in his parents' arms, listening to them paint word-pictures, a child learns that reading feels good. When the time comes, he will want to recreate this feeling for himself.

Third, parents should read to themselves. Children follow the examples set by their parents. If parents read, children will, in all likelihood, follow suit. If, on the other hand, parents rely on the television as a primary source of entertainment and information, so will their children.

There are two things parents *should not* do if they want their children to become successful readers:

First, they should not teach a preschool child such things as the alphabet and how to read unless the child specifically *asks* to be taught. Even then, take a casual approach, and if the child loses interest, leave well enough alone. Studies have repeatedly demonstrated that the "head start" produced by preschool reading programs only lasts a few years.

Second, parents should not let preschool children watch more than a few (that's three!) hours of television a week, if any. Increasingly, researchers are finding that children who spend disproportionate amounts of time watching television during their formative years have more reading problems than children who watch very little. A child watching television is not exercising *any* of the skills he or she will eventually need in order to become a successful reader. Experts are now saying that this lack of appropriate developmental exercise and stimulation, accumulated during hours and hours of television watching, can permanently impair a child's reading ability.

Chapter Six

When to Medicate

"**I**s my child hyperactive?" is a question frequently asked by parents of children with learning and behavior problems.

Over the last twenty-five years or so, the term "hyperactivity" has become slang. It is loosely, and more often than not, *inaccurately* applied to children who are active, strong-willed, and difficult to control.

Hyperactivity is actually one aspect of a larger set of problems known as Attention Deficit Disorder, or ADD. Attention Deficit Disorder is a relatively common childhood syndrome with both neurological and behavioral features. As the term implies, ADD children have short attention spans and a correspondingly high level of distractibility.

ADD children distract themselves as often as they are distracted by things going on around them. For example, if an ADD child is working on a puzzle and one of the shapes in the puzzle reminds him a picture he recently saw in a magazine, he might leave the puzzle to look for the magazine. By the time he finds the magazine, he's forgotten about the puzzle. As he flips through the magazine, something other than the picture for which he was looking catches his eye. He's soon forgotten why he started looking through the magazine in the first place.

This inability to "screen" distractions, both external and internal, is thought to be due to a slight malfunction in the child's central nervous system. Comparing the child to a radio, it's as if the child's "tuner" isn't working. Instead of being able to lock into one station and stay there indefinitely, the child "drifts" randomly and involuntarily from station to station.

Another way of explaining the disorder is to say that the ADD child's central nervous system appears to be "out of tune." I often compare the child's brain and spinal cord to the engine and drive train of an automobile. Just as a perfectly good engine, if out of tune, will perform poorly, the ADD child's central nervous system is structurally normal but "out of tune" due to a minor chemical imbalance. As a result, it will not support an adequate attention span.

Their short attention spans and distractibility cause ADD children to have difficulty concentrating on and completing assignments in school. A vicious cycle develops: As the child falls further and further behind in his school work, he begins to lose interest. As motivation declines, he pays less and less attention in class and completes fewer and fewer assignments. Even highly intelligent ADD children, by the time they reach third grade, are usually lacking in both academic skills and motivation.

An unusually high activity level (hyperactivity) may be present, but isn't essential to the diagnosis. While truly hyperactive children always have attention deficits, some ADD children are not hyperactive.

Fine-motor coordination is often a problem as well, resulting in poor handwriting. Because they have difficulty organizing information, ADD children tend to be forgetful and have problems following directions. The manner in which ADD children approach tasks is generally haphazard, and their rooms and desks at school are usually in a state of confusion.

The ADD child's problems at school usually parallel problems that already exist at home. According to their parents, ADD children are generally restless and unable to occupy themselves for significant periods of time, consistently interrupt conversations, seem to crave the center of attention, rarely finish chores, and seem "immune" to traditional forms of discipline. Because activity tends to be impulsive, rather than goal-directed, ADD children tend to "bounce" from activity to activity, rarely completing anything. They tend to be argumentative, generally oppositional, and continue throwing tantrums long after most children have stopped.

One of the most common and infuriating aspects of an ADD child's behavior is the seeming inability to accept responsibility for any wrongdoing. Their parents frequently report that even if they're seen "in the act," they will deny having done anything wrong.

These behavior problems are the logical consequence of poor impulse control. When hyperactivity is involved, the combined effect of impulsivity and a high activity level creates behavioral chaos, and discipline will be an almost constant problem for parents and teachers. The child is likely to be especially active and disruptive in public places, such as restaurants and stores, where structure is lacking and the level of stimulation is relatively high.

Many ADD children have difficulty getting along with peers. They have as much difficulty following rules as they do following directions, which brings them into frequent conflict with other children. They tend to have problems sharing and playing cooperative games, and their low tolerance for frustration causes them to become quickly angry or tearful if games don't go their way. As a consequence, other children tend to become quickly alienated from the ADD child; therefore, ADD children are very likely to complain a lot of being shunned and picked on.

If this description fits your child, you should request an appointment with either your child's pediatrician or a child psychologist. Because the syndrome involves both neurological and behavioral features, it is important that treatment of the ADD child always be coordinated between a physician and psychologist, both of whom should be thoroughly familiar with the syndrome and experienced at treating it.

Questions?

Q: What is the cause of Attention Deficit Disorder?

A: There is not *one* cause, but many. Various studies have implicated heredity, maternal diet (including alcohol consumption, drug use, caffeine use, and smoking) during pregnancy, food allergies, and developmental (maturational) problems. Most researchers agree that the syndrome can best be understood in terms of interactions between social, psychological, and biological variables.

Q: What does treatment usually involve?

A: The most effective treatment approach is *multi-modal* in nature, involving not one, but a combination of therapies. Many ADD children, especially those with mild forms of the syndrome, can be managed using traditional methods, including behavior modification and remedial education. For others, medication becomes very helpful, but only if used along with behavioral and academic strategies.

The most frequently used medications are Ritalin (methylphenidate hydrochloride), Cylert (pemoline), and Dexedrine (dextroamphetamine sulfate). These medications chemically stimulate the central nervous system, putting it back "in tune." As a result, the ADD child is better able to screen distractions and focus attention on a single task until it's been completed. Impulse control and, therefore, tolerance for frustration also improve, as do overall organizational skills.

Once they've been started on medication, many ADD children, and especially those with hyperactivity, are observed to be less active and disruptive. As a consequence, many people mistakenly believe that these medications are tranquilizers, or have a paradoxical tranquilizing effect on ADD kids. To set the record straight, Cylert, Ritalin, and Dexedrine are *stimulants*, not tranquilizers. They energize the central nervous system in a way that enhances the child's attention span. Because these medications assist the ADD child in focusing on a single task for a longer time period, his or her activity level comes down considerably. This lowering of activity is not, however, due to the chemical action of the medication, but is actually a positive side-effect. Furthermore, these medications will lengthen just about anybody's attention span. You wouldn't notice any difference, however, in a child whose attention span is adequate to begin with.

It's important to realize that while these medications enable a longer attention span and better impulse control, they have no magical capacity to suddenly cure the behavioral, motivational, and academic difficulties that inevitably develop over the course of time. Rather, by resolving the neurological aspects of the disorder, these drugs allow a clearer "shot" at the child's behavioral and academic problems. Medication should never—I repeat *never*—be used as the sole method of treatment.

Q: What kinds of tests can be given to determine whether or not a child has Attention Deficit Disorder?

A: Despite the claims of some professionals, there are no clinical, psychological, or medical tests that will diagnose ADD. The diagnosis is based on observations of the child in structured and unstructured settings, information obtained from teachers and parents, a developmental history, and school records. Although it's not diagnostically necessary, many clinicians, including myself, routinely obtain measures of IQ and academic performance skills. Many ADD children are found, upon evaluation, to have learning disabilities. Regardless, they're almost always behind in school and require academic remediation to one degree or another.

Q: After a child is started on medication, how long does it take before it takes effect?

A: That depends on the medication. Cylert must accumulate to a certain level in the bloodstream before it produces any results. This generally takes two to three weeks. With Ritalin and Dexedrine, however, results are generally immediate and, as the following story demonstrates, can be fairly dramatic.

A few years ago, I saw a six-year-old, first-grade boy who was having learning and behavior problems at school. In the course of my initial evaluation, I asked his teacher to provide me with a written description of the problem.

She wrote: "Brendan is in almost constant motion throughout the day. He will roll on the floor, get up suddenly and begin walking around the room, move his head rapidly from side-to-side, drop things on the floor, and talk to himself. In addition, he chews almost incessantly on pencils, crayons, and his clothing. Brendan never raises his hand, talks out-of-turn a lot, and much of what he says has nothing to do with whatever discussion is taking place. Needless to say, he will neither start a task nor stay with it unless I 'stand over him.' I've tried everything I know to help Brendan control and modify his behavior, but there's been no change. When I isolate him to one end of the classroom, he is somewhat better. To tell the truth, however, that benefits me and the other children more than it does Brendan."

Frustration flows from the pores of that letter, don't you agree? That was in early December. I helped Brendan's parents and teacher implement several behavioral strategies designed to assist him with self-control, but he showed little improvement. Over the holiday break, therefore, I asked Brendan's pediatrician to start him on a trial of Ritalin, which he did, beginning with a small morning dose. Brendan had no adverse reaction to the medication, so just prior to the resumption of school I asked the pediatrician to increase the morning dose slightly. Around the middle of January, I obtained information from the teacher which, although generally encouraging, indicated that Brendan's behavior took a turn for the worst around noon. This was predictable, given that Ritalin "wears off" after about four hours. I then asked the pediatrician to prescribe a second small dose to be administered at 11:30 in the morning. In the meantime, we continued with the behavioral interventions, which were now beginning to "take hold."

At the end of February, I received a second letter from the teacher. She said: "There's been an almost complete turnaround! Brendan is more focused, and his attention span has increased tenfold. He's staying with tasks until they're complete and is sometimes even going beyond what's expected of him. In addition, he is beginning to show signs of being able to apply what he's learning in the classroom to new tasks and situations. I've also noticed that letter formation and spacing have greatly improved. During instruction and class discussion, Brendan is far more composed. He's still anxious to participate and make comments, but goes about doing so in appropriate ways. He attends to his book bag and school belongings without direct reminders from me and no longer chews on his clothing or other items. Brendan is making tremendous social progress, as well. His aggressive behavior toward peers is subsiding and is presently at a level that I consider typical for boys this age. The other boys and girls are beginning to seek him out to play, and he seems much more at ease with them and much better able to give and take."

While both the medication and behavioral interventions played significant roles in Brendan's turnaround, the degree of change described by the teacher could never have been achieved with either medication or behavioral methods alone. In this case, the medication simply opened a "window of opportunity" that enabled the behavioral interventions to begin working.

Q: Our eight-year-old son was recently diagnosed as having ADD with hyperactivity. The diagnosing psychologist referred us to our pediatrician, who started our son on Ritalin, which he takes before school. The psychologist and pediatrician both minimized the potential of possible side effects, but we have since learned Ritalin can be quite dangerous. They insist, however, that our son isn't taking enough medication per day to warrant concern. Do you agree?

A: Not exactly. Any time a child is given a drug, the risk of side effects is enough to warrant concern. Perhaps the better question is, "Should you be *worried*?" To that, the answer is an emphatic "No!"

Ritalin, along with every other drug, involves a certain amount of risk. Literature published by its manufacturer, Ciba-Geigy Corporation, lists nervousness, insomnia, headaches, abdominal pain, skin rash, and tachycardia among a number of possible adverse reactions.

Psychotic episodes have been associated with abuse and overdose. There have been scattered reports of growth suppression with long-term use, but a clear cause-effect relationship has yet to be established. Also, clinical studies have suggested that Ritalin and other central nervous system stimulants can result in the onset of a severe multiple tic disorder known as Tourette's syndrome. But believe it or not, Ritalin has fewer and less serious possible adverse reactions than probably ninety percent of the medications listed in the *Physician's Desk Reference* (PDR). It has never, to my knowledge, been associated with a child's death or permanent impairment.

In the final analysis, Ritalin is a relatively benign drug, as are Cylert and Dexedrine, the two other medications used in treating attention deficit disorder. They pose less risk, in fact, than aspirin, which has caused numerous childhood deaths.

The typical therapeutic dose for a grade-school child is between 10 and 20 milligrams per day, usually administered only on school days. Within those limits, the most likely side effects include a temporary suppression of appetite, difficulty in getting to sleep, minor headaches, and slight stomach distress. If properly prescribed and monitored, a child stands virtually no chance of ever becoming drug-dependent, psychologically or otherwise.

It's true that Ritalin has been the recent target of a lot of bad press. I suspect, however, that in many of the horror stories attributed to it, Ritalin serves as a convenient scapegoat—a simplistic way of explaining an otherwise complex situation that has more to do with family dynamics than chemistry.

That isn't to say that Ritalin has never been abused professionally, because it definitely has. There have been hundreds, perhaps thousands, of cases in which Ritalin has been inappropriately prescribed. Several years ago, for example, I saw an eight-year-old whose physician had prescribed an initial dose of 30 milligrams of Ritalin a day solely on the basis of an isolated report from a teacher that the child was daydreaming in class. The physician had not taken pains to check out the report or verify it with other teachers, past or present. Not only was the diagnosis inappropriate, but the dosage was two to three time the normal trial level! The child reacted with mood swings, irritability, sleeplessness, and a markedly lowered tolerance for frustration. The parents stopped giving the Ritalin after about a week, and the child immediately returned to normal. I shudder to think of what might have ensued otherwise.

Despite dramatic stories such as this, Ritalin is a relatively benign and immensely helpful medication. Like any other drug, its helpfulness depends upon proper diagnosis and prescription. Theoretically, improper use of Ritalin, especially over a long period of time, could contribute to the onset of emotional problems, including violent and perhaps even self-destructive behavior. Used conservatively and in combination with behavior therapy, however, the chances are slim that the child will suffer any long-term adverse effects.

When I was a child, there was always a bottle of penicillin—then considered a "wonder drug"—in our refrigerator (one of the "advantages" of having a stepfather who worked part-time as a pharmacist). Every time I'd get the slightest temperature, my mother would pull out the bottle and medicate me every four hours until all hints of illness was gone. At age twenty-nine, after taking penicillin for a minor throat infection, various parts of my body began to swell and itch. Within minutes, I looked like the Pillsbury Doughboy. My wife rushed me to the emergency room, but by the time we got there, the allergic reaction had subsided. The doctors told me, however, that if I ever take penicillin again and am not within fifteen minutes of a hospital, I'll probably die. Does my "horror story" (and many others like it) mean that penicillin is a bad drug? Of course not! My allergy is the result of unintentional misuse, not an inherently bad medicine.

The same is true of Ritalin. If attention deficit disorder is properly diagnosed, and Ritalin is prescribed cautiously and monitored properly, there's virtually no need for worry. Most of the potential side effects pass within a week or two. Nothing to get excited about. Long-term adverse effects can be kept in check by giving the child regular "vacations" from the medication.

Drugs such as Ritalin should be used with respect for the risks involved. But the bottom line is this: They've helped thousands of children make the best of their abilities in school. It would certainly be a tragedy if that became lost in a haze of hysteria and misinformation.

Q: For the past year, we've been seeing a psychologist for help with our son's unruly behavior. He's helped us with a discipline plan, and Robbie's behavior at home has improved tremendously. Things at school, however, weren't getting any better, so after making a diagnosis of ADD, the psychologist asked Robbie's pediatrician to start him on Ritalin, to be taken only on school days. Robbie's behavior and performance at school have been steadily improving ever since. We recently switched pediatricians, and the new one wants Robbie on the Ritalin seven days a week, rather than just school days. He says this is more effective. In our opinion, Robbie doesn't need the medication on weekends, especially since the discipline plan is working so well. What's your opinion?

A: This happens to be a topic of debate within the pediatric community. Some pediatricians think Ritalin should be used only on school days since, in the majority of cases, problems in school led to the diagnosis. They also tend to think that instead of using Ritalin as a "crutch," parents should rely upon improved disciplinary methods to control the child's home behavior. This argument has a lot of merit, particularly if the child's problems are more evident at school than at home.

Other pediatricians argue that children with ADD need as much help with their attention span and impulse control on weekends as they do on school days. They feel, therefore, that the medication should be given every day. There is also merit to that position, especially if the child is having a real struggle with self-control at home.

In my opinion, the issue turns strictly on the severity of the problem. A child with a relatively extreme case of ADD, and especially if hyperactivity is involved, may initially need the medication every day. Meanwhile, the child's parents should be receiving guidance in behavior management from a psychologist. Once effective disciplinary controls have been established at home, I think it's best to have the child off medication on nonschool days.

Parents often report that Ritalin doesn't seem to result in any observable change in their children's behavior when they're at home. This is because Ritalin's effect is more pronounced and noticeable in a task-oriented environment, such as a classroom. In a less structured setting, you're less likely to see any change in the child's outward behavior. Parents who aren't employing prescribed behavior modification techniques at home, because they're not capitalizing properly on the opportunities the medication affords, are also unlikely to notice any change in the child's behavior.

Even when the prescription calls for medication on school days only, parents may discuss with the pediatrician the option of giving the medication selectively on nonschool days when the child is going to be in church or some other equally structured situation.

In your case, I would ask the psychologist to intervene on your behalf with the pediatrician. If he's assured that things are going well on weekends, he will probably relax his "seven days a week" rule.

Q: What kinds of discipline work with ADD children?

A: The same kinds that work with other children. With non-ADD children, however, parents can afford a slightly greater "margin of error," in terms of inconsistency, than they can with ADD kids.

In other words, ADD children don't require different discipline, they just require more of it. Remember that ADD children have more difficulty with impulse control, otherwise known as self-discipline. Because they step "out of bounds" more often, it is of utmost importance that their parents realize the importance of making rules clear and enforcing them consistently.

For specific suggestions on setting up the kinds of family and disciplinary structures that work for both ADD and non-ADD kids, I suggest you read my last book, *John Rosemond's Six-Point Plan for Raising Happy, Healthy Children* (Andrews and McMeel, 1989).

Q: I teach third grade and, this year, have two ADD children in my class, both of whom, even though they're on medication, are hard to handle. The school psychologist recently told me that they were not able to control their behavior and should not, therefore, be held personally responsible for whatever problems they cause in the classroom. Instead of punishing them for inappropriate behavior, she said I should reward them frequently for good behavior. Any other approach will damage their self-esteem. I thought I was hearing things, but when I asked for clarification, she repeated exactly what I thought she'd said. Do you agree with this?

A: Absolutely not! The school psychologist obviously means well, but she's mistaken. ADD children must be held completely responsible for their own behavior. That's the only way they're ever going to develop adequate self-control. The one thing they don't need, under any circumstances, is excuses being made for them by people like your school psychologist—people whose thinking is clouded by an excess of sympathy. Sympathy drives compensatory responses which, as I've already pointed out, do not serve to correct problems and, in the long run, only make problems worse.

If a misbehaving child—ADD or not—isn't held responsible for his own behavior, he has no chance of ever changing it. Being held responsible by others helps the child eventually accept responsibility on his own. Accepting responsibility for one's own behavior is the essence of self-control, which is part and parcel of self-sufficiency—the ability to stand on one's own two feet—which is the essence of self-esteem. Holding a child responsible for his own behavior, therefore, leads to improved self-esteem.

Concerning the suggestion that you reward these kids often for good behavior, I would simply point out that reward-based disciplinary strategies don't work. First, because children saturate on any given reward fairly quickly, any changes in behavior brought about by reward-based strategies are generally short-lived. As the child's interest in the reward wanes, so does the improvement in behavior. Second, rewards don't move responsibility toward the children in question. The people accepting responsibility for maintaining good behavior on the part of the child are the people who must constantly dish out for the rewards.

Third, rewards prevent children from learning that appropriate behavior is desirable for its own sake. Instead, rewards instill a "what's in it for me?" attitude toward good behavior. None of this is compatible with helping children develop good self-esteem.

For specific suggestions concerning classroom management, read Chapter Three.

Q: My husband and I are seeing a psychologist because of discipline problems with our six-year-old son. Charlie has also had problems in school this year; namely, concentrating and finishing work. The psychologist recently told us that part of Charlie's problem is attention deficit disorder. We're confused. If Charlie has such a short attention span, then how can he sit quietly and watch television for two or three hours at a stretch?

A: The fact that Charlie can watch television for two to three hours doesn't contradict a diagnosis of ADD. Television holds Charlie's interest in a way the everyday world doesn't— *can't*—because the picture on a television screen changes every few seconds.

Not only is the television's flicker highly stimulating, it also has a mesmerizing, or hypnotic, effect upon the viewer. This is television's "hook," created through the use of anywhere from three to five cameras in the production studio. Some people seem better able to resist the bait than others, but children are especially susceptible. Furthermore, television's constant flicker doesn't require a long attention span. In fact, the change of perspective every few seconds is perfectly suited for a child with ADD.

Although television keeps Charlie quiet, it's actually making his attention span problems worse, rather than better. While watching television for three hours, he's not watching any *one* thing for longer than about ten seconds, four seconds being the norm. In other words, television-watching actually *reinforces* Charlie's short attention span. The longer he watches, the more his short attention span becomes habit.

For these reasons, I always recommend that ADD children be allowed no more than three hours of television a week. Furthermore, this should consist primarily of shows like nature documentaries, where content, rather than production technique, is the element holding the child's interest.

Q: How long does an ADD child have to take medication?

A: The average length of treatment on medication for ADD children in my practice is two years (with summers off), but when I recommend medication, it is but one part of a multi-modal treatment plan that includes building a structured framework of discipline (rules and consequences) and responsibility (chores) in the home as well as educational therapy (tutoring) to remediate academic performance deficiencies that may have accumulated. The younger the child is when the disorder is diagnosed, the earlier treatment is started, the more effective the communication and coordination between parents, psychologist, pediatrician (or family practitioner), and teachers, the shorter the length of treatment on medication. As I said before, medication only opens a window of opportunity on the behavioral and academic problems that develop around this neurological disorder we call ADD. Under normal circumstances, that window only needs to be propped open with medication for about two years. At that point, assuming significant progress has been made and the child's condition has stabilized, medication can usually be discontinued. The behavioral and academic facets of the treatment program, however, must be continued indefinitely.

Q: Do ADD children ever "outgrow" the disorder, or is it with them for life?

A: There is much controversy and relatively little consensus on this issue among the professional community. Some believe children outgrow the disorder in adolescence. Others believe that while symptoms may lessen with age, traces of the disorder can be detected throughout the individual's lifetime.

I subscribe to the view that ADD is a developmental disorder with both neurological and behavioral features. At the core of the disorder is the neurological dysfunction—an "out-of-tune" central nervous system. As the child matures through adolescence, the neurological disorder probably begins to correct itself. In other words, the core begins to shrink, perhaps to eventual insignificance. However, if the behavioral and academic features of the disorder have not been successfully remedied by this time, they will continue to cause the individual significant problems. In this sense, without treatment, the problems caused by ADD do remain with the individual indefinitely.

Q: Can ADD children be treated successfully without using medication?

A: If the disorder is detected early enough in the child's life, if parents diligently apply themselves to creating the kind of structure needed in the home and elsewhere, and (this is the kicker), if the child is exhibiting a relatively mild form of the disorder, then there is significant likelihood that the child can be treated successfully without using medication.

As ADD children grow older, their symptom pictures tend to become more complicated. Even so, older ADD kids, even those with fairly severe forms of the disorder, can be treated without medication. The risks, however, are great, and I wouldn't recommend taking them.

When he was a youngster, our son, Eric, exhibited all of the symptoms of ADD. Unfortunately, because I was also young and inexperienced, and because not much was known about the disorder at that time, I did not recognize his problems as such. We suspected that he was "hyperactive," but I was adamantly opposed to using medication with children. I thought these medications (Ritalin and Dexedrine) were just a lazy person's cop-out, and that giving them to children was a form of child abuse. So, we struggled for years to get control of Eric and help him get control of himself. Fortunately, we were successful. Today, he is a high-achieving, self-motivated, mature, personable adult. I can't say enough good things about him. However, although there are no scars (at least none of which I'm aware), the emotional toll on all of us (Eric in particular) was great and, in retrospect, largely unnecessary. In short, if I had it to deal with all over again, I wouldn't hesitate to have him take medication. I'm now certain that it would have made our lives—particularly his—a lot easier.

Q: Our ten-year-old, fifth-grade daughter has ADD along with a learning disability. As a result, school is very difficult and frustrating for her. She spends part of every school day in a special program for children with similar problems, but her progress has not been what we initially hoped it would be. On a recent television talk show, we heard a psychologist who specializes in treating learning disabled children say there was a relationship between food allergies and learning disabilities, including hyperactivity. What can you tell us about this?

A: Over the last twenty years or so, there's been growing interest in the effect of diet on children's behavior. Quite a number of people, lay and professional alike, believe that allergies and "sensitivities" to certain foods and/or food additives cause neurological stress which, in turn, gives rise to hyperactivity, learning disabilities, and other childhood behavior disorders.

Elimination diets—so called because certain foods and food additives are subtracted from the list of allowed foods— have attracted a large number of devotees, most of whom are parents who claim that one or another of these diets virtually cured their hyperactive and/or learning disabled children. The most well-known of these diet plans is the Feingold diet, named after its physician-developer. Although carefully controlled research has consistently failed to confirm the Feingold diet's curative powers, numerous parents—as well as some physicians and psychologists—remain convinced of its benefits.

Sugar has been another substance of controversy. Again, many parents, along with some professionals, claim that sugar causes an increase in activity and irritability, along with a decrease in attention span in certain "sugar-sensitive" children. Conversely, they believe that restricting the sugar intake of ADD and LD children will improve their behavior and school performance. Research has failed to substantiate these claims, as well.

Indeed, one occasionally hears of a child whose problems disappeared after sugar and/or food additives were removed from his diet. While there's no reason to doubt the truth of these stories, there are other ways of explaining the supposed "cures." Studies have shown, for example, that the simple act of paying attention to someone in any systematic way is likely to bring about improvements in that person's behavior.

From both a nutritional and dental standpoint, it makes good sense to limit the amount of sugar in a child's diet. It's also wise to keep the number of processed foods in a child's diet to a minimum. However, the research indicates that neither sugar nor food additives seem to deserve the reputations they've acquired as behavioral villains.

Epilogue: Building Solid Foundations

Traveling around the country, making presentations and conducting workshops for parents and professionals, I'm asked many questions on a full range of topics related to the raising of children. One question frequently asked by parents of preschool children is, "Are there things we can begin doing *now* to prepare our child for success in school?"

I answer, "The single most important thing you can do is teach your child the "Three R's."

The reaction is almost always the same. At first, they stare at me with puzzled expressions. When they're certain I've said all I'm going to say, they ask, "But isn't that what teachers are for?"

"Ah, yes," I reply, "You're referring to the "Three R's" of reading, 'riting, and 'rithmetic. Indeed, that is what teachers are for. I'm talking, however, about the "Three R's" of respect, responsibility, and resourcefulness. Every child should come to school already equipped with a well-established attitude of respect for adult authority, a practiced sense of responsibility, and a talent for resourcefulness. That's a parent's job. If, and only if, parents will do their job, can teachers do theirs. Likewise, teachers *cannot* do what parents have failed to do."

Respect for Authority

In order for one person to learn something from someone else, that person must figuratively "look up" to the other. Without respect and admiration for the teacher's knowledge and authority, the student will not learn much of value. At best, he may absorb lots of facts, but the likelihood is he will not be able to put them to much use.

Likewise, a child who does not come to school with a previously established respect for authority is not likely to become an effective learner. He will not understand why it is important for him to pay attention to the teacher or do what she tells him to do. He may also bring behavior problems with him to school that further interfere with his ability to put his intelligence to good use.

He will probably interpret his teachers' attempts to discipline him as indications they don't like him. His parents, neither able nor willing to see their role in his problems, may even support this view. As he progresses through the grades, his attitude toward his teachers, and the educational process as a whole, will probably become increasingly cynical. In his mind, school will become a battleground of "me against them."

His inability to understand the value of an education may lead him to drop out of school as soon as he is able. Regardless, he'll probably drop out mentally sometime around junior high school. When he enters adult society, his disdain for authority, for the system, will follow and cause him untold problems throughout his life.

Not a pretty picture, is it? For that reason, it is essential that parents fulfill this important obligation to their children— that of teaching them to be respectful of themselves and other adults.

A respectful child pays attention in class, is eager to please his or her teachers, is curious, participates in class discussions, looks for ways of doing more than just the minimum, obeys the rules, and learns, learns, learns.

To teach a child respect, parents must first center the family around themselves. This means that in a two-parent family, parents should pay more attention to their marriage than they do the children. In a single-parent family, the single parent must, for her children's sake as well as her own, pay slightly more attention to herself than she does her children. If this sounds heretical, as if I'm advocating some subtle form of neglect, it's only because many people have been seduced by the "children come first" mentality that our society has come to sanction.

A family should not, *must* not, revolve around the presence of children. Children should orbit around the *adult* presence in the family. This state of affairs helps children divest of self-centeredness, which is essential to developing a respectful attitude toward adults. It also says to the children, "You are expected to pay attention to us."

You *do* want your children to pay attention to you, don't you? Then you *must* occupy the central, most prominent position in your family. You cannot expect your children to pay attention to you if you act, day in and day out, as if your most pressing obligation is that of paying attention to *them*. It will not, cannot, work both ways, and the choice is yours.

The unwritten understanding between parent and child should be, "When I, your parent, want your attention, you have no option other than to pay attention to me. However, when you want attention from me, I will decide whether it is prudent and necessary to give that attention to you." In other words, the parent has a choice, the child does not.

Unfortunately, in many families, this fundamental dictum has been turned upside-down and inside-out. Many parents act as if they are obligated to pay attention to their children whenever their children want attention, and especially if they demand it. Today's parents seem to believe that if they deny their children attention, they will make them insecure. This belief was handed down from on high by a number of so-called experts who wrote books about childrearing, and it has since become solidly entrenched in our culture.

The myth is that children need a lot of attention, that the more attention you pay a child, the more you inflate his sense of self-esteem. The truth is that infants need a lot of attention, toddlers need a lot of supervision, and children require less and less of either as they grow. Self-esteem has little to do with how much attention a child receives from his parents and everything to do with how much his parents encourage self-sufficiency. Parents who pay too much attention to their children maintain, if not increase, their children's dependency.

As my mother used to say, "Children are not here for parents to cling to, and parents are not here for children to cling to." Parents are here to help children move slowly but surely out of their lives and into lives of their own. That is the sum total of a parent's trust, the responsibility one assumes when one chooses to activate one's child-making equipment.

To teach a child respect, parents must also expect obedience. This expectation must be clearly stated in order to be clearly heard. If, and only if, parents truly expect obedience will children be obedient.

The years since World War II have seen parents become increasingly confused concerning how to properly raise children. Much of this confusion was manufactured by experts who marketed to an unsuspecting public such absurd and altogether destructive notions as the "democratic family" and the "child-centered family." These experts took the realities of parenthood and replaced them with rhetoric. They took the common-sense of raising a child and replaced it with nonsense. In the process, they undermined the confidence of nearly an entire generation of parents, who began to feel as if they had no authority other than that which their children would accept, which was little, if any.

So, instead of expecting obedience, which the experts had told them they had no right to do, parents began wishing for it. This wishful thinking takes the form of pleading, bargaining, bribing, threatening, haggling, haranguing, and most of all, arguing with children.

Unfortunately, children don't grant adult wishes. When their wishes don't come true, parents become frustrated and complain about their children's behavior. Sometimes they complain to the children themselves, who, if the truth were known, are not impressed. Or these parents pound on the table, get red in the face, and threaten terrible, unthinkable horrors if the children do not immediately obey. This results in temporary obedience, and further loss of true respect.

"Respect your child," said the experts. "Remember that respect is a two-way street. Your child will respect you only if you show respect for your child." This was part of the rhetoric of the democratic family, a family in which everyone lives in harmony because no one is in control. *Everyone* runs the show. Children are regarded and treated as equal to adults and are, therefore, consulted concerning any and all decisions that might affect their little lives. And everyone lives happily ever after. That's the myth.

Here's the truth: Children need parents who are constant in their demonstrations of competence and self-confidence. Children need parents who act as if they are powerful enough to protect and provide for them under any and all circumstances. Self-confident parents instill confidence in their children, and this confidence anchors a child's sense of security and frees that child to begin exploring the limits of his or her own potential for competence.

Children need parents who know where they stand and stand firm. If parents stand in one place one minute and in another the next and yet another the next, it becomes impossible for their children to become convinced of their ability to protect and provide for them. These parents are unreliable, and unreliable parents make for insecure children. Their insecurity drives what is called "testing behavior," which is nothing more than an anxiety-ridden search for where their parents stand.

The child who constantly tests is really asking, "Please stop moving around, because every time you change positions, every time you are inconsistent, every time you say one thing and do another, every time I am able to wear you down by whining and pleading, every time you give in to one of my tantrums, I am forced to test that much more."

Parents who are inconsistent engage their children in a perpetual game of hide-and-seek, and the fact that their children have no choice but to play consumes enormous amounts of their developmental energies—energies that would otherwise be available for creative pursuits, for self-expansion, for activities that bring success. Testing never brings success. It is not possible, therefore, to test and feel good about yourself at the same time.

I agree that parents should show respect for children. I also agree that respect in the parent-child relationship is a two-way street. But the traffic that moves from parent toward child is and must be vastly different in quality from the traffic that moves from child toward parent. You see, children show respect for parents by obeying them. And parents show respect for children by expecting them to obey.

In my last book, *John Rosemond's Six-Point Plan for Raising Happy, Healthy Children* (Andrews and McMeel, 1989), I promoted what I call "The Power of 'Because I Said So.'" The book hadn't been out four weeks when I received a letter from a reader in Albuquerque, New Mexico, complaining that when she was a child, "because I said so" was her parents' answer to everything. That experience undoubtedly and understandably left a bitter taste in her mouth for those four words, and she chided me for giving parents permission to use them, saying, "Children need to know the reasons behind the decisions parents make."

I agree that, operating as they did out of a "children should be seen and not heard" mentality, many of our parents used "because I said so" to put us in our place and get us to shut up. Behind the "because I said so" was the implied threat that if we didn't bite our tongues, serious consequences would be forthcoming.

But whereas those four words may at times convey a rigid, unreasonable attitude, they are not, in and of themselves, unreasonable. I'm not advocating a repressive, totalitarian form of parent government, nor do I have a problem with parents telling children the whys and why nots behind their decisions.

I happen to be fairly old-fashioned when it comes to raising children. I believe that the primary function of being a parent is that of acquainting children with reality and helping them toward self-sufficiency. It's a reality that, even in a democratic society, authority figures—teachers, lawmakers, employers—frequently make and impose arbitrary decisions. Somebody decides things are going to be done this way rather than that way, that the line is going to be drawn here rather than there, that the standard will be based on this measure as opposed to that one, and so on. Why? Because that particular somebody or body of somebodies said so. And having said so, the rest of us have to live with it, at least until some other authority comes along and arbitrarily decides something different.

Likewise, approximately four of every five parental decisions are founded on nothing more substantial than personal preference. When that's the case, "because I said so" (or a variation on that theme) is the most honest answer. Not snarled, mind you, but clearly and calmly stated.

I believe parents have a responsibility to confront that reality with their children. Unfortunately, partly because "because I said so" was crammed down our throats and partly because nearly an entire generation of self-appointed parenting "experts" arbitrarily decided that "because I said so" was a no-no in the parent-child relationship, today's parents don't feel they have permission to say those four words, or variations upon them, to their children.

By and large, today's parents feel they are obligated to explain themselves to their children. Furthermore, they seem to believe that their explanations must satisfy and pacify the children. Consequently, those explanations take on a persuasive, pleading, even apologetic, character. Implicit to this is the absolutely absurd idea that parents don't have a right to enforce a decision unless (a) it can be supported by reasons other than personal preference; (b) the children understand those reasons; and (c) the children agree with them.

Now hear me clearly. I'm not saying that parents should never give reasons to children; I'm saying that parents should make no attempt to *reason* with children, and there is a big difference. Reasoning is the futile attempt to persuade a child that your point of view is valid. Face it, our children will understand our points of view when they themselves are parents, and no sooner. That's the way it always has been, and always will be.

If you want to explain yourself, then by all means do so. But don't expect the child to agree. When he doesn't, simply say, "I'm not asking you to agree. If I was your age, I wouldn't agree with me either. You have my complete permission to disagree, but you do not have *any* permission to disobey."

In other words, the child does what he's told not because his parents succeed at providing an explanation that smooths his ruffled feathers, but simply because he's been told. So, you see, even in the act of giving reasons, the bottom line is still "because I said so."

Responsibility

School is a responsible environment. To the degree that children come to school primed with responsibility, they will accept the responsibilities expected of them by their teachers. A teacher cannot instill a sense of responsibility in a child, she can only capitalize on what is already there.

The most effective means of priming a child for responsibility is to assign him or her a regular, daily routine of chores around the home. Children should begin doing chores no later than age three. At first, they should be responsible simply for picking up their toys, keeping their rooms orderly, and clearing their own plates from the table. As they grow, their responsibilities should extend into "common" areas of the home. By the time a child is of kindergarten age, he or she should be practiced at sweeping, dusting, running a vacuum cleaner, taking out garbage, setting and clearing the table, helping with the washing and drying of dishes, and making his own bed. Outdoors, a five-year-old is fully capable of helping with raking, sweeping, weeding, and watering.

Chores are important because they are a child's only means

of making tangible contribution to the family. Acts of contribution, performed on a regular basis:

> • Bond a child to the family and its values. For proof of this, ask yourself, "Where in America have family values and traditions been handed down most stably and reliably from generation to generation?" The answer, of course, is in rural areas of this country where, not coincidentally, it is normal for children to participate in the work of their families from an early age.
>
> • Actualize the child's membership in the family. All acts of contribution are acts of participation. To the extent the child participates in the life of the family, the child's membership is acknowledged and affirmed. That affirmation imparts a sense of security to the child that cannot come as well from any other source.
>
> • Give the child a sense of value and worth. Chores are a means of accomplishment for a child. Every opportunity for accomplishment is an opportunity to develop self-esteem, and self-esteem is addictive, which simply means that a child with self-esteem will seek ways of adding to it through—that's right!—accomplishment.
>
> • Teach important domestic skills. As such, chores enhance self-sufficiency and further strengthen self-esteem.
>
> • Prepare children for good citizenship. John F. Kennedy gave Americans the perfect prescription for responsible citizenship when he said, "Ask not what your country can do for you; ask what you can do for your country." For a child to eventually become a good citizen of this country, he must first be a good citizen of his family. To accomplish this, parents must teach their children that it is better to seek ways of doing for the family than to expect the family to constantly do for them.

Considering all of the above, there is absolutely no excuse for not expecting children to perform a regular, as in daily, routine of chores in and around the home. Unfortunately, there are more children in this country who do *not* contribute to their families on a regular basis than there are children who do. Parents rationalize this failure in a number of ways:

They say, "It's more of a hassle to get the kids to do something around the house and do it right than it is for us to do it ourselves." This is a cop-out of the first magnitude.

They say, "What with all of the after-school activities they're involved in, there's no time for our children to do much work around the house." This is a cop-out of the second magnitude.

They say, "We believe childhood should be a relaxed, carefree time, not filled with responsibilities. We feel that expecting them to do well in school is enough." This is a cop-out of the third magnitude.

They say, "There really isn't that much for the children to do around the house because we have both a cleaning service and a yard service that come in once a week." This is a cop-out of the fourth magnitude.

In the first place, it is indeed worth the hassle, which will be short-lived if parents will simply take a stand on the subject of chores and stand firm.

In the second place, if a child is involved in so many after-school activities that he has no time to do chores, then he's involved in too many after-school activities. It's a simple matter of priorities—first things first.

In the third place, a child who is responsible around the home will be more responsible at school. He will be a better all-around student because he will bring to school a stronger desire for accomplishment.

In the fourth place, do your children a favor and save yourself some money by letting the cleaning service and the yard service go!

I'll be blunt. A child can either be a participant in the family or a parasite. A parasite is an organism that attaches itself to another, usually larger, organism and derives benefit from the relationship while contributing little, if anything, of value to it. It is a "something for nothing" proposition, and "You can get something for nothing" is the powerful message sent to a child who is not a fully participating member of his or her family.

The idea that something can be had for nothing is a false-hood, but a child who has lived within the fantasy that's im-plicit to that falsehood is very likely to bring that fantasy to school. He is likely to believe that education, like everything else that's ever come his way, is something someone *gives* you. This, of course, isn't true. Education, like self-esteem, is some-thing you *get*, something you work for. Someone may extend to you the opportunity, but whether you take advantage of the opportunity or not is strictly a matter of choice.

How do you want your child to choose?

Not expecting a child to be responsible around the home sets the stage for homework battles. The "something for noth-ing" child isn't likely to be any more active a participant in his education than he is in his family. His teachers will report that he won't work unless they stand over him, rarely participates in group discussions, and seems to not care whether he makes good or bad grades. Is that any surprise? A child's attitude toward responsibilities at school is simply an extension of what is or is not expected of him at home.

The "something for nothing" child will come home with work that should have been done in class, and he will work as hard to avoid doing the work as he did at school. Maybe harder, for home is where the "something for nothing" lesson was learned in the first place, and where "something for noth-ing" behavior has worked in the past, more often than not.

Every evening, the "something for nothing" child's par-ents will sit with him at the kitchen table and prod him along until his homework is finally done. Here, as elsewhere, they will end up doing too much for him, and once again he will get something for nothing.

And the beat goes on.

Resourcefulness

According to my dictionary, a resourceful person is one who uses his or her "fullest capacity for finding, adapting, or inventing means of solving problems." School is a problem-solving environment. It stands to reason that the more resourceful a child is, the better a student he or she will also be.

The resourceful student will be far less likely to cash in his chips when confronted with a difficult problem than one who is not so equally endowed. To a resourceful child, a difficult problem presents simply another opportunity to explore, experiment, adapt, and/or invent, all of which bring pleasure, in and of themselves. The resourceful child is able to think more flexibly, more creatively. His ability to examine any given situation from a variety of perspectives means he is more adept at trial-and-error, the essence of "if at first you don't succeed, try and try again."

Resourceful people enjoy being challenged. They love to clear hurdles and are always looking for higher ones. If they fall short of their goals, they become that much more determined. Resourceful people regard dejection and despair as a waste of time. In short, resourceful people are the winners of the world.

If you want your child to become a winner, then I have three radical suggestions:

First, say "No" to his requests more often than you say "Yes."

"No" is the most character-building two-letter word in the English language. Children who hear "no" sufficiently often learn to tolerate frustration. This tolerance enables them to persevere in the face of obstacles and adversity, and perseverance—need I remind you?—is the essential ingredient in any success story. Whether the pursuit be vocational or avocational, social or spiritual, perseverance makes the difference between those who consistently reach their goals and those who don't. It may sound strange to say, but if you want to help your child develop a successful attitude toward the challenges of life, you must not be afraid to frustrate him.

Part of the problem here is that many, if not most, of today's parents dedicate themselves to making their children happy. They give too much to their children and require too little. As a result, the children begin to believe that happiness is achieved through the process of acquiring things. Like their parents, they confuse self-esteem with happiness, and whatever self-esteem they manage to develop is but a shadow of the real thing.

In order to equip a child with the skills he will need to pursue happiness on his own, the skills he will need to achieve success in life, parents must be courageous enough to make that child occasionally and temporarily unhappy. In order to help a child learn to stand on his own two feet, parents must not prop him up with one material thing after another.

It's important that parents know the difference between what children truly need and what they simply want. It then becomes important that parents give children all that they truly need along with a conservative amount of what they simply want. This prudent conservatism forces a child to figure certain things out for himself. In effect, his parents are saying, "We won't figure everything out for you." Under the circumstances, he has no choice but to become more ingenious, more adaptable, more inventive, creative, and self-reliant. More resourceful.

Second, buy your child very few toys.

Another way of looking at this issue of resourcefulness is to say that a resourceful person is able to do a lot with relatively little. In 1952, when I was five years old, I had five toys. That wasn't unusual. It was, in fact, the norm. My toys were a set of Lincoln Logs, a set of Tinker Toys, an electric train, a small set of lead calvary and foot-soldiers, and a cap-pistol.

Compare this with the number of toys the average five-year-old of today has in his or her possession. One hundred? Maybe two hundred? More? And yet, parents tell me that today's children complain of being bored more than they complain of anything else. This is new. Boredom was something I didn't know as a child, and I wasn't alone.

I've asked countless numbers of people who raised children in the forties and fifties, "Did your children frequently complain of being bored?"

"No," is their answer. Always.

Why not? Because when we were children we didn't have a lot of toys. We had to learn, therefore, how to do a lot with relatively little. And that's what resourcefulness is all about.

Whenever I run into an individual who taught school from the early fifties to at least the late seventies or early eighties, I ask, "How would you compare the children you taught late in your career with those you taught early in your career?"

Invariably, they tell me that latter-day children are less imaginative, less creative, possess less initiative, and are less— you guessed it—*resourceful* than children were in the "good old days."

That should tell you something.

Third, don't let your children watch much television, especially during their preschool years.

This is where I attempt to persuade you, the reader, that television really *does* rot the brains of small children. I don't mean that literally, of course, but I *do* mean that regardless of the program, "Sesame Street" included, it wastes their precious time.

Nearly every human being is born already programmed for intelligence, creativity, and an incredible variety of other skills. During the formative years, these skills are activated by exposing the child to environments and experiences which "push the right genetic buttons," so to speak. Releasing the richness of each child's developmental birthright simply requires that he have sufficient opportunity for exploration, discovery and imaginative play. Environments and experiences which stimulate and exercise these emerging skills are, therefore, compatible with a growing child's developmental needs, while environments which fail to offer these important opportunities are incompatible.

Consider how television fits into this relationship between environment and development. The average American child watches more than five thousand hours of television during his preschool years, much more time than is spent in any other single activity. In effect, television has become a primary environment for America's preschool children and must therefore be impacting greatly upon their development.

The question then becomes, "What competency skills are being exercised as a child watches television?"

The answer: None.

Watching television doesn't engage or involve visual tracking, active problem-solving, fine or gross motor skills, social skills, communication, inquiry, exploration, initiative, motivation, imagination, creativity, or achievement. Furthermore, because of the incessant "flicker" of a television screen, watching television doesn't help a child develop a long attention span. These are, incidentally, the skills that a child must bring to school in order to become a successful reader.

The developmental skills that comprise and support the act of reading are acquired during the preschool years in the course of the most natural of childhood activities, play. Television-watching is neither a natural nor playful activity. In fact, it is not an activity at all, but a *passivity*. It is a deprivational experience that masquerades as "fun."

Evidence that television has taken its toll on the competency and literacy of America's children can be found in the fact that since 1955, when television became a fixture in nearly every American home, academic achievement at all grade levels has declined and learning disabilities have become epidemic. It is not at all coincidental that a list of learning disability symptoms closely parallels the aforementioned list of deficiencies inherent in watching television.

For all these reasons, I think it would be ideal if children were not exposed to any television—even "Sesame Street"—until they were successfully literate. Once a child learns to read and enjoys reading, however, it becomes appropriate to let him watch programs that expand and enrich his understanding of the real world, programs such as nature and wildlife specials, documentaries about other countries and cultures, sports events, programs about space exploration, and so on. Programs of this sort stimulate a child's curiosity and interest, and the intellectually curious child is more likely to ask to be taken to the library.

I'd shout it from the rooftops if I could be certain the guys in white jackets wouldn't come, truss me up in a stainless-steel straitjacket, and take me away in their portable rubber room. Instead, I talk about it at every possible opportunity because I believe, more than I believe just about anything else, that every child has an inalienable right to become as complete and competent as he or she was meant to become.

A couple of years ago, I said it to an audience in Charlotte, North Carolina. Several months later, I received a letter from one of the parents who'd been in that audience.

She wrote: "Although skeptical that you could convince me that watching 'Sesame Street' is harmful, I went with an open mind. Enclosed is a photo of my two daughters, taken several months ago while they were watching television (the photo showed two children, ages four and two, sitting mesmerized in front of a television).

She went on to say, "I was always proud of their ability to sit and watch PBS children's programs by the hour. I thought that since they had never seen a commercial and only watched 'educational' programs, they would be unscathed.

"My husband and I returned home from your lecture and turned off the television. None of us have seen a program since. What amazes me is how we don't miss it at all, and also how much more time we have available to us. Toys that hadn't been touched since last Christmas are now being played with daily. We read more stories and enjoy our time together more since our lives no longer revolve around the television listings. Thank you for changing our lives."

Lest the reader think this mother's experience is unique, I've heard the same thing from many other parents.

After attending one of my presentations, a mother in Waterloo, Iowa, wrote, "Because what you said was so consistent with what my husband and I had observed of our two-year-old daughter's behavior when she watched television, we established a 'no television' policy in our home. We noticed an immediate increase in Rachel's speech and language skills. In four months, she went from two-word utterances to singing entire songs and retelling, along with acting out, her favorite stories. I'm a skeptic no more! As a speech therapist, I don't believe Rachel's skills would have developed so rapidly had we continued to let her watch television an average of two hours per day, as she had been doing before we heard your talk."

Testimonials like these have convinced me beyond a shadow of a doubt that television-watching pacifies the growing child's intellect and imagination and interferes significantly with the development of social, perceptual, motor, and language/communication skills.

So, turn off the television and turn on your child!

In Closing . . .

There's been lots of talk lately about the need for parents to become supportively involved in their children's education. As a result, parents are asking, "How *should* we get involved, and how can we best demonstrate our support of education?"

In answer to that question, I recently heard an educator say that parents should visit their child's classroom on a regular basis. He said they should establish a "presence" in what he called "their child's primary learning environment."

That's interesting, I thought to myself. In the first place, a child's primary learning environment is the home, not the school. In the second, regardless of how often they visit, and even if they never visit at all, parents *do* establish a "presence" in their child's classroom. Every day a child goes to school, he takes his parents with him, in the form of their discipline, their expectations, and their values. And the child's performance in school reflects that presence—the degree to which his parents have succeeded in preparing him for the responsibilities his teachers will expect of him.

I have a slightly different answer to the question of involvement: The best way to get involved, the best way to support the efforts of your children's teachers, is to put first things first. At home, concentrate on building strong foundations for learning and excellence by teaching the "Three R's" of Respect, Responsibility, and Resourcefulness. As I said before, teachers cannot do what parents are supposed to do. They can only *capitalize* on what parents have already accomplished and are continuing to reinforce.

A child's education is a two-handed process. On the one hand are responsibilities that belong to the schools. On the other are responsibilities that belong to the child's parents. Only by joining hands will the child's education be truly complete. And only if those hands are joined will the child be able to accept those responsibilities that belong to him.

About the Author

Family psychologist John Rosemond is Director of The Center for Affirmative Parenting (CAP), located in Gastonia, North Carolina. CAP is a national parent resource center whose primary activity is that of providing workshops and other educational presentations for parents and professionals who work with children and families. CAP also provides print and audio materials on parenting and child development.

Since 1978, John has written a nationally syndicated parenting column which currently appears in close to one hundred newspapers across the United States and Canada. He is also the regularly featured parenting columnist for *Better Homes and Gardens* magazine.

John's last book, *John Rosemond's Six-Point Plan for Raising Happy, Healthy Children*, was published by Andrews and McMeel in 1989 and was, after only nine months, in its fifth printing. His first book, *Parent Power! A Common-Sense Approach to Raising Your Children in the Eighties*, was published by East Woods Press in 1981 and Pocket Books in 1983. *Parent Power!* is currently out of print, but is scheduled for re-release by Andrews and McMeel in the spring of 1991.

In 1981, John was selected "Professional of the Year" by the Mecklenburg County Mental Health Association of Charlotte, North Carolina. In 1986, he was presented with the Alumni Achievement Award by his alma mater, Western Illinois University.

Throughout the year, John is in considerable demand as a

public speaker. His parenting presentations and workshops have drawn high marks from parent and professional groups all over the country.

Last, but by no means least, John is husband to Willie and father to Eric, twenty-one, and Amy, eighteen.

Anyone interested in contacting John may do so by writing him at The Center for Affirmative Parenting, P.O. Box 4124, Gastonia, North Carolina, 28053, or calling him at (704) 864-1012.

If you found this book useful, you'll be happy to know there are more from John Rosemond, America's most widely read parenting authority.

Rosemond is the author of a series of parenting books from Andrews and McMeel. In addition to *Ending the Homework Hassle*, two more books are available at your local bookseller:

John Rosemond's Six-Point Plan for Raising Happy, Healthy Children

Rosemond's critically acclaimed bestseller is a guide for creating a family that brings out the best in every family member. The book is an affirmation of common sense that will free parents from the child-centeredness that is undermining today's family.

The Six-Point Plan is also available as a three-hour audio-cassette tape series (not a reading of the book), and is an excellent tool for stimulating family and group discussions (the book serves as the leader's guide).

Parent Power! A Common-Sense Approach to Parenting in the '90s and Beyond

Parent Power! is chock-full of practical, common sense solutions to problems encountered by parents of children of all ages.

Rosemond's approach in *Parent Power!* is developmental and problem-oriented. In it, he helps parents identify and understand the significance of each stage of a child's growth, anticipates the problems typical (and in some cases, not-so-typical) to each stage, and provides workable advice for resolving those problems.

Parent Power! was first published in 1981 by East Woods Press and was a Main Selection of the Young Parents Book Club in that year. It was later released in paperback by Pocket Books. This new edition has been revised and updated to include chapters on teenagers, adoption, bedtimes battles, and divorce and custody. The developmental section has also been greatly expanded to cover a broader range of issues and topics.